80s Guys

RESTAURANT AND ARCADE

A Book by Ryan Taylor Ed.D.

Dedicated To

Tamarah, Lexie, Rhett, Lilie, Tyce, and Trey

Also, my best friend Rod and of course the eighties

Thanks to my family and friends who inspired me and tolerated my shenanigans in the eighties

Edited by: Nicolle Brown (Short Stuff)

Table of Contents

Chapter One: Growing Up Hooper 3

Chapter Two: Becoming Young Men 8

Chapter Three: College and the Dating Scene 16

Chapter Four: Navigating Relationships 27

Chapter Five: The Next Step 32

Chapter Six: First Sign of Adversity 39

Chapter Seven: How Could Elvis Do This to Us? 44

Chapter Eight: The Aftermath 51

Chapter Nine: The Nineties Suck! 59

Chapter Ten: The 80s Guys 70

Chapter Eleven: A Good Place 76

Chapter Twelve: Progressing 81

Chapter Thirteen: Again? 86

Chapter Fourteen: We Used to be Hermits 94

Chapter Fifteen: First-Time Customers 112

Chapter Sixteen: Life is Good 120

<u>Chapter One: Growing up Hooper</u>

Rand Brooke and Ross Fraser had known each other their entire life. Their families had been close even before they were born. They played on the same blankets as infants and fought over the same rattle. Growing up, there was never a time when they were not best friends.

The two boys would make an interesting experiment because they were so alike in many ways. Their fathers were cousins, making them second cousins. They were born two months apart and grew up just a mile away from each other. As members of the Church of Jesus Christ of Latter-Day Saints, they were in the same ward, same scout troop, same grade in the same school, same friends, and they played on the same sports teams. So, were they similar because they were related or because of growing up in the same environment? Some would say a little of both.

When Rand and Ross entered kindergarten at Hooper Elementary, they had the same speech problem. They both had trouble saying their Rs. The two palled around, calling each other Wand and Woss. Some sessions with a speech therapist learning to place their tongue at the roof of their mouth to say rooster over and over soon alleviated the speech issue. However, the two nicknames playfully stuck with most of their family and friends.

In their early years, the two loved adventures, and Hooper was a great place to find them. Hooper is a farming community located just east of the Great Salt Lake in Utah. The fields in Hooper grow corn, sugar beets, onions, and peas. The pastures had horses, cows, pigs, goats, and even the occasional buffalo.

Rand lived on the last road in Hooper. The walk to the shores of the Great Salt Lake was close to a quarter of a mile. Ross lived about a mile away, so during the summertime, it was an easy bike ride to the other's house. During the school year, they both rode the same bus, so after school, they took turns getting off at each other's bus stop. The fields and pastures, along with the Great Salt Lake, made for plenty of opportunities to find adventure.

A field not yet prepared to plant seeds made for a great place to find dirt clods. Dirt clods meant dirt clods fights. Rand and Ross did not need Nerf guns like today's youth. These clods were bigger, messier, and hurt worse than the foam bullets played with today.

One unforgettable day they had in their earlier years was when they discovered a field of mud after a rainy day. The two boys recruited Ross's younger brother Shane to participate in a football game on the field of brown sludge. After the game, the threesome hobbled back to Ross's house with mud dripping from head to toe because of the large clumps they had tackled each other in. It took several minutes for Ross's mom to spray the boys off with a garden hose before they were deemed clean enough to get in a bath to finish the job.

The Brooke and the Fraser families both loved to go camping. During the summer months, the two families, along with several other family friends and relatives, would set off for Montana, Idaho, Wyoming, or Utah's Uintah Mountains in their truck and campers. There was always at least one motorboat between the families that could be used for lake fishing during the campouts. Rand and Ross both pulled many rainbow trout out of Hebgen Lake in Montana near Yellowstone National Park. When they were not fishing, the two boys were usually found on their bicycles riding along the dirt trails with their pocketknives, looking for the next adventure.

Rand and Ross were both very competitive, even at a young age. One summer morning, while they were searching for the next escapade, they came across a bull in a small corral just down the road from Rand's house. Ross dared Rand to run across the corral. Rand had just got a new pair of sneakers and was eager to try them out, so he looked at the bull. He did not think it was too scary, so he decided to accept the challenge. So, he climbed the wooden fence of the corral and only took one step towards the other side when the bull rose from its mini-sleep and began charging towards Rand. Rand suddenly realized how intimidating the bull was, after all. He got to the other side of the corral just before the bull, but he still needed to climb the fence. Luckily, he saw a gap at the bottom, slid feetfirst underneath the fence, and safely made it to the other side.

At this point, the bull was truly mad. He glared at Rand for a while and then went back to his corner of the corral but did not lie back down. Rand and Ross were now standing on opposite sides of the corral with the bull looking on as if he was baiting the boys to try that again. He glanced over at each boy, waiting for one of them to hop the fence in hopes of making it to the other side. Ross looked over at Rand and thought, if he can do it, then I *must* do it as well.

Ross waited for the bull to look Rand's way, and then he climbed the fence. It took a second, but the bull noticed Ross's movement. Then, he turned around and started after Ross, with his head down and nostrils flared. Ross knew it was going to be a close call. He decided to slide headfirst through the gap like one of his favorite baseball players, Pete Rose. Unfortunately for Ross, there was a cowpie right at the spot he was heading for with no time to adjust his course. He slid headfirst into the cowpie under the fence and came up on the other side with the front of his shirt covered with cow manure. They were both safe now but would have some explaining to do to their mothers.

Beating the bull gave Ross and Rand additional confidence to compete in the Little Buckaroo Rodeo starting in the third grade. The rodeo was held at Ogden's Golden Spike Arena, and several different events inspired little buckaroos to someday be full-grown rodeo competitors.

The two boys both entered the calf-riding competition. Those calves may not have been bulls yet, but to Rand and Ross, they were plenty big. Ross won the calf-riding competition in the third and fifth grades, with Rand taking second in both years. Rand won the calf-riding first-place buckle in the fourth and sixth grades, with Ross taking second in both years. As competitive as the two were in those days, if one of them got the better of the other one day, it was almost always returned the next.

Besides rodeo, Rand and Ross competed in football, basketball, and baseball. No matter which sport they played, they always worked well together. Ross was the quarterback throwing the ball to Rand, the wide receiver. They both played basketball, excelling in shooting, dribbling, and occasionally passing. In baseball, they were interchangeable as shortstop and pitcher. Their teams were successful mostly due to the two of them. They both needed to win to satisfy their competitive thirst, and they did throughout their little league days.

Rand and Ross both liked to fish. Ross was a great fisherman. Rand was not so bad a fisherman; he caught plenty of fish, but he had bad luck much of the time when he fished. One example of this bad luck was on a scouting trip when Rand walked behind a fisherman who was casting a giant lure on the line. When the fisherman cast his rod forward, the hooks in the lure caught Rand in his bare leg, and the hook was embedded in his thigh.

Two of Rand's scout leaders performed minor surgery involving needle-nose pliers and wire cutters to get the hook out. The hook had to be pushed all the way through the skin, and then the prongs had to be clipped off before pulling the hook back out. Ross stood by for moral support. The fisherman's lure was ruined, which he made sure Rand was fully aware of. The experience ruined Rand's day, and he made sure the fisherman knew this as well.

One of Rand and Ross's favorite accomplishments happened in the summer after fourth grade. It was their first year of fast-pitch baseball, and their team, the Hooper Blue Jays, won the Roy City and Weber County championships. In the county championship, the Blue Jays defeated the Hooper Dodgers, the other Hooper team in this age group. Their basketball team, the Hooper Falcons, also won several championships during Rand and Ross's early years of playing sports.

Rand and Ross enjoyed life. They had a way of making things fun for everyone. They both had a good sense of humor, and they used it constantly. A lot of kids made fun of others to get a laugh, but this was neither Rand's nor Ross's style. They had fun, but not at the expense of others.

Chapter Two: Becoming Young Men

Ross and Rand started Roy High School in 1982. The two boys were both nervous and excited about the idea of high school. Much like other boys their age, they were excited to play sports and meet new girls. However, they were a little nervous about playing sports against older, bigger, and stronger boys.

The two boys were both solid students in junior high school and continued that trend in high school with B+ to A- averages. Ross excelled more in English and Science, and Rand more in Math and History. They were also not a problem for teachers or administrators. They were a dream to have in class. They never got into any serious trouble. Much like their early years, Ross and Rand's high school years were full of fun and good experiences.

Once the boys turned sixteen at the end of their sophomore year, they began to date. Neither boy had a steady girlfriend in high school. Instead, they did a lot of group dating. Most of their dates came from a group of girls with similar interests and values. It was not uncommon for Ross to take a girl to the movies with a group that included Rand, and a month later, Rand took the same girl bowling in a group with Ross. Likewise, Ross would do the same with someone Rand had recently been out on a date with. The two enjoyed dating without getting serious. Also, by not having a serious relationship, they could concentrate on their true love, which was sports.

Ross and Rand caught the sports bug early in their lives. Attending Weber State games with their fathers was a big part of learning to love sports. Playing sports and competing is what drove the two. Ross and Rand played basketball, baseball, and football throughout high school.

Ross was the better basketball player, Rand the better baseball player, but they both excelled at all three.

Never getting too serious with a girl also helped Rand out in another way. He got incredibly nervous around girls that he did not know well. Rotating through a group of girls helped Rand relax. This group of girls were his friends, so Rand was better able to control the nerves. However, dances like Homecoming and the Prom were a bit more difficult.

During a girl's choice dance in his senior year, Rand's nervousness resulted in some serious stomach issues. Intestinal gas was building up, and he did not think his date would appreciate him breaking wind. Rand confided in a friend, Steve London, that he was struggling with his stomach and could not hold his "bottom burps". Steve lets Rand in on a little secret to tell his date that he hears something in the engine, and he wants to check it out. This would score some points with his date because he handles the car issue, and she need not worry. This would also get him out of the car so that if he needs to blow off some steam from his bowels, he could let it loose outside. Rand tried it on the way home, and it worked like a charm.

Ross and Rand both loved listening to music. Pop and Rock music were their favorites. Music would relax them and also energize them. Roy High would hold stomps often after games. A stomp was an informal dance. If Rand met a girl at a stomp, his nerves would be fine. If he met a girl at a pizza restaurant without music in the background, his stomach would be a mess. The eighties music soothed Rand's stomach.

Besides getting the nervous jitters around girls, a big part of Rand's stomach issues was his eating habits. He drank a lot of soda and ate a lot of candy and fried foods. It was common for Rand to stop at the Hooper Store on his way home and purchase potato logs, chicken fingers, mini burritos, and Swedish fish for dinner. He would wash it down with a drink from the soda fountain. He almost always bought a vitamin pack as well. This way, Rand thought he was getting plenty of nutrients along with the fried and starchy food.

What he was getting was a weak stomach. Situations that would make anyone nervous were exacerbated by the ingredients in Rand's stomach. Sometimes, Rand did not need a nervous situation to have stomach issues.

One summer morning before Ross and Rand's junior year, the two arrived at Roy High early for a weightlifting session. They were the first two in the weight room, so they went to the back of the room to work on the bench press machine. Suddenly, Rand felt his infamous stomach episodes coming on. He had ingested some packaged muffins, a soda, and a pack of vitamins from the store that morning for breakfast. It was a typical breakfast for him, but this morning, it was not sitting well.

Rand was grabbing at his gut. Ross politely asked him to go to the other side of the room and let out the air biscuits that were building up in his stomach. Rand obliged by walking slowly over to the front door. Within seconds, Rand let it go. Then again, and again, and again. He was tooting more than the trumpet section in Roy High's marching band. Rand finally said, "I better head over to the restroom." He then left the weight room.

Ross was glad he was on the other side of the room. At least until coaches and teammates started filing in. Each coach and teammate walked into the weight room through the front door and immediately smelled what Rand had left in his wake. Then they saw Ross at the back of the room and reasoned that it must have been Ross who had generated that smell.

Everyone who walked in the door left within seconds, holding their hand over their nose. A few even became nauseous from the smell. This went on for about ten minutes.

Rand returned from the bathroom to find the entire football team and coaching staff standing outside of the weight room. Rand walked past them and began to re-enter the weight room. One of the coaches spoke up and said, "You do not want to go in there. Ross has stunk the whole place up." Rand replied, "I am sure it's fine now." Another coach commented, "Those two spend so much time together they are used to each other's farts." That brought a laugh from the team.

Rand entered and found Ross still at the back of the room. Ross was unhappy, but he knew Rand had not intentionally set him up. Rand told Ross, "I will let them know it was me." Ross quickly replied, "Thanks, bud." Rand opened the door and announced, "It smells like B.O. again, guys, instead of a nasty fart, and by the way, it was me and not Ross who is guilty of smelling up the room." The announcement was met with several "Yeah rights." Coach Fernandez, who the boys had known since they played on his tee-ball team after the second grade, told Rand it was nice of him to try to cover for Ross. Rand tried to convince coaches Jay Green and Blaine Thompson that it really was him. They just smiled and shook their heads, and the team went about their business. "Thanks for trying," Ross said.

Ross and Rand's families also had strong friendships with each other. Ross's mom, Lorraine, used their strong bond to help Ross overcome a nasty habit. Ross constantly chewed at his fingernails, and he had been biting his nails for several years. It was to the point that he had little fingernails left. Lorraine was tired of Ross ruining his fingernails, so she gave Rand permission to smack Ross whenever he saw him biting them.

It only took about a half-hour for Rand to utilize his new authority. Rand saw Ross biting his nails and smacked him hard on the back of his head. "Dude! What are you doing?" Ross asked, quite perturbed. "Your mom said that I could smack you when you were biting your nails," Rand replied. It took less than a month and several headaches, but Ross quit his horrible habit.

Ross and Rand graduated from Roy High in the Spring of 1985. At the age of 19, boys could serve missions for the Church of Jesus Christ of Latter-day Saints, and they both desired to do this. However, Ross would not turn 19 until March 1986, while Rand's birthday was in May of that year. So, they decided to go to Weber State College for a year before departing on their missions.

That year was awkward for both. They were continually meeting new girls, but they did not want to have serious relationships because they would be leaving on their missions for two years. As that first year of college continued, they decided to date less and less as they got closer to leaving on their missions. Also, most of their friends had earlier birthdays and left before Ross and Rand. The two of them discovered the pool tables in Weber State's Union Building, so they spent a lot of time hanging out there talking about their future.

Ross received his mission call in February and learned he would be leaving in early June, right after the end of Spring Quarter at Weber State. Ross would be serving in Caracas, Venezuela. Rand's call came in March, and he learned he would be leaving in late July for Buenos Aires, Argentina. They both would be learning Spanish. Ross's last week in the Missionary Training Center (MTC) would be Rand's first week.

Giving up two years did not seem like a giant sacrifice for Ross and Rand. They had a great love for the Savior and a testimony that the true church was the Church of Jesus Christ of Latter-Day Saints. They both read their scriptures every day and prayed fervently that their testimonies would continue to grow. They would miss their families and friends, but Ross and Rand were both very excited to depart on their missions and serve for two years.

Ross and Rand would try to find each other whenever possible during the week they spent together in the MTC. They were able to eat together a few times and play basketball together, but they always found one another at the end of the day. They looked forward to that short amount of time spent together and used it to have spiritual discussions.

One night, Rand told his companion that he was heading over to a friend's room and left him with their other roommates. Unfortunately, Rand's companion did not hear him say he was leaving and where he was going. Rand and Ross had a wonderful spiritual discussion that night in the stairwell just outside Ross's room. The two were so enthralled by the scriptures they were sharing with each other that they lost track of time. It was well past curfew when they realized how late it was.

Rand walked back to his dormitory, but the doors were locked. Luckily for Rand, his room was on the bottom floor of the dorm. He walked over to the window of his room, peeked in, and noticed his other three roommates were kneeling in prayer. Rand folded his arms and waited for his roommates to finish. When the prayer was over, Rand said, "Amen," and knocked on the window. His companion ran to the window to find Rand peeking in.

The roommates immediately ran to open the front doors of the dorm. After returning to their room, they told Rand how worried they had been and thought he had decided to leave the MTC. They decided to say a prayer in the hope that Rand would stay on his mission and return to the MTC. Immediately after their prayer, they heard the knock and saw Rand.

Rand looked at his companion and said, "I told you I was visiting my friend Ross. Did you not hear me?" Rand's companion shook his head no. The roommates were slightly deflated because they thought they had prayed Rand back to the MTC, but then they found out it was only a lack of communication.

When the boys headed to South America, they stayed in contact with each other. They wrote letters to each other regularly. The letters were spiritual-based and shared scripture, much like the discussions in the MTC. Besides writing letters, they both had devices that recorded on cassette tapes, which they used sometimes instead of writing letters. They would talk on the tapes and send them home so their family members could hear their voices occasionally. They also sent tapes back and forth to each other.

They found ways to get tapes from Argentina into Venezuela without anyone opening and stealing the contents in their mail. Rand had his mother send some Pringles chips in his care packages along with some duct tape. Pringles come in a tube. Rand would eat the chips, put the cassette tape along with some candy in the Pringles tube, and then duct tape it securely. Taking apart the thick duct tape was too much work for anyone thinking about opening and stealing the contents, so it became an effective way to get mail into Venezuela. Venezuela had one of the world's worst mail systems.

During these two years, as the boys became men, they also discontinued using the word dude. Dude had become their favorite word, and they used it often and in many ways. For two years, they would learn not to say the word dude. However, if they had found an equivalent word to dude in Spanish, they would have most likely used that word often.

The men came home from South America a little over a month apart in the summer of 1988. They had both become fluent in Spanish and had grown immensely during their missions. Ross and Rand both loved teaching the Latin people. They loved teaching the Gospel. They had grown in their testimonies of the Savior, His Atonement, the Restoration of the Gospel, and the Prophet Joseph Smith. As they returned home to Hooper it was now time for a new chapter in their lives.

<u>Chapter Three: College and the Dating Scene</u>

Newly returned missionaries Rand and Ross were ready to move on to the next phase of their lives. They both made plans to attend Weber State College for the Fall Semester of 1988. Rand decided to major in history, while Ross majored in English. They both wanted to teach at the high school level and probably coach as well. They each decided to get jobs, and Rand started at Pro Image, a sports paraphernalia store in the Ogden City Mall. Ross worked with his uncle in the landscaping business.

Even more than attending college again, Rand and Ross were excited to get back into the dating scene. Almost immediately, Rand and Ross were approached by relatives, ward members, and friends who said they had the perfect girl for them to meet. The thought of blind dates did not appeal to either of them at this point. Rand's nervousness and subsequent stomach issues were much better after becoming comfortable approaching strangers and asking them questions about life and religion for two years. Still, a blind date was more than he wanted to even think about.

Rand and Ross were twenty-one years old and didn't need to hurry up and get married. The two wanted to meet girls organically and see what happened. Even Rand, with all his nervous jitters, thought it may be fun to date as a recently returned missionary. Life was good.

In 1988, 90% of students at Weber State were commuters. Ross and Rand were part of that ninety percent. Rand and Ross had three or four classes depending on the day of the week, but no classes together other than an Institute class, where they continued to grow their testimonies in the Church of Jesus Christ of Latter-Day Saints. A typical day for the two was to arrive on campus around eight in the morning, make it to their first class by 8:30, after attending different classes, they would meet for lunch at the Union Building at 12:30, and then head for either work or home. Rand usually worked nights at the Pro Image, and Ross worked afternoons for his uncle.

Lunch in the Union Building was Rand and Ross's favorite time of the day during the week. Their friends from high school, Ralph, Lyle, Jody, and Farrell, would usually be there as well. The group would discuss their latest dates, sports, and what they had learned in their classes. Typical stuff for young men that age. After lunch and some discussion, whichever boys did not need to get to work right away would head downstairs, where there were pool tables, a bowling alley, and an arcade. Most of the time, they would play a few rounds of pool, but they also bowled or played their favorite video games like Galaga, Asteroids, and Donkey Kong. Rand and Ross did not have a lot of difficulty in their lives. Life was good. But it was about to become stressful, unbeknownst to them.

Besides the Union Building, Rand and Ross spent free time at the Institute Building across the street from Weber State. It was just a short walk from the Social Science Building, where many of their classes were held. Rand and Ross had an institute class together on Tuesday nights called "Preparing for an Eternal Marriage." They thought the class might be a great way to meet girls. They also often attended the Tuesday Devotional, Sunday Fireside, and the Friday Night Activity (FNA) at the Institute.

The FNA in late November of that Fall Semester would lead to a stressful and awkward situation for Rand and Ross. That week's activity was a dance after a Weber State home basketball game. During the dance, they both danced with several girls. For most of the night,

Rand and Ross were in eye contact with each other, but at the end of the night, they had become separated. When the dance ended, they found each other in a hallway that led out to the rear parking lot. They were both excited to tell the other about one of the girls they had danced with. Just then, Ross saw the girl he had been dancing with walking out of the back door, and he wanted to show her to Rand.

Ross blurted out, "Look! There is Cindy right over there!" The two boys headed for the back door, but there was a lot of people traffic between them and that back door as people filed out of the dance. It took Rand and Ross a couple of minutes to make it to that back door. When reaching the parking lot, Ross scanned around, looking for Cindy. Finally, he spotted her in the passenger seat of an orange Volkswagen Jetta exiting the parking lot. "There she is!" Ross yelled as he pointed in the direction of the Jetta. Rand turned and saw the girl but quickly had a nauseous look on his face. "That is not Cindy. That is Sandy and the girl I danced with as well." Stunned, Ross said, "I could have sworn she said her name was Cindy."

The two boys made their way to Rand's pickup truck. They both looked as if their dog had died. They both had been so excited about this girl. When they got inside the pickup cab, they both said to the other almost simultaneously, "Go ahead and date her." Then they both cracked a smile and knew they could never do that to the other.

Cindy or Sandy, whatever her name was, had long blonde hair. She was tall, about 5'9, and slender. She had a great smile with beautiful blue eyes. Neither Rand nor Ross told their other friends about the girl they had danced with at the FNA. They both kept thinking of her but didn't mention her to each other much. There was a little bit of tension there because of this. When she did come up, it was one telling the other that they couldn't believe they had both fallen for the same girl. They would laugh it off, but both wished the other had never danced with her.

The late November FNA was the last one for the Fall Quarter. Finals came and went. Rand and Ross were both excited about the results of their report card. They were both better students since they had come home from their missions. Now, they could relax and enjoy their first Christmas home from their mission. However, neither Rand nor Ross could get that FNA girl out of their head.

Ross had been companions with the son of Utah's Governor while in Venezuela. He invited Ross to a New Year's Eve party at the Governor's Mansion. Ross asked Rand to come along. It was a lot of fun, and they both met some interesting girls. Still, if one of them found themselves speaking to a girl that they had seen the other speaking with, they held back. Not wanting there to be a repeat of the FNA back in November, neither Rand nor Ross wanted to be too charming. They both left the Governor's Mansion that night feeling like they had blown a great opportunity to meet someone new. They did not want to upset the other, but should they hold back? Were they missing out on other great opportunities? They had already backed away from one girl for each other. Should they continue to hold back from any girl the other had met or talked with? Rand and Ross were both asking themselves these questions.

The winter quarter began, and Rand and Ross both had schedules like those of the fall quarter. Three or four classes a day and then meet for lunch in the Union Building. There was not much landscaping to do with snow on the ground, so Ross did not have any work to do for his uncle. However, Ross had made enough during the summer and fall that he was not worried about money.

Rand was still working at the Ogden City Mall. Ross would come down to the mall about once a week. On Rand's break, they would head to the food court. One night in January, Rand had to get back to the Pro Image and left Ross to finish his pizza slice. Then, Ross noticed a girl sitting by herself at the next table, so he decided to be brave and sit by her, and they had a great conversation.

The next day, Ross told Rand about Tamara from Copper Rivet, whom he had met at the food court. Rand, with a sullen face, said, "Yeah, I know Tamara. We have dinner a lot in the food court. We usually have a break at about the same time." It had happened again. Ross thought maybe he should tell Rand to go for the FNA girl, and he could ask out Tamara. His thoughts continued, why has he not told me about Tamara? Is it because he likes her? Maybe he wants to ask her out, and then I could ask out the FNA girl.

Tension was growing between Rand and Ross, although neither discussed it. They continued to celebrate each other's accomplishments and support each other in their disappointments, but this was something they had never dealt with as friends before. How could they work this out and make it fair to both?

Even though neither boy was pursuing the FNA girl, she had not left either of their minds. During the winter quarter, they both constantly ran into her on campus, but never when the other was around. Neither mentioned to the other when they had seen her. Rand and Ross would always just say hello to her and nothing more. Her reaction was never consistent with Rand or Ross. One day, it could look like she wanted more than just a hello, and she thought they had made a connection at that Friday Night Activity. She gave a look as if to say she was interested and confused as to why that interest was not returned. The next day, it looked like she did not know him, and she wondered why he was saying hello to her.

One day in early February, Rand and Ross were playing pool with their other friends in the Union Building. Rand left to use the restroom. Before he got to the restroom, he saw the FNA girl exiting the girl's restroom. Rand had always wondered if her name was Sandy, as he thought, or if it was Cindy, as Ross thought. Rand thought to himself that it was time to find out. Rand looked over at the FNA girl and said, "Hello, Sandy." The FNA girl had that quizzical look on her face as if she did not know why he was saying hello to her, but then she smiled and said, "I am not Sandy. I am Cindy." Rand said to himself, "Crap! Ross was right." She then said, "Sandy is my sister."

Rand nearly fell to the ground. "Wait, you have a sister named Sandy?" Yes, an identical twin sister named Sandy," she explained. It was starting to make sense to her now. "We thought you two knew we were identical twins. We have been wondering why neither of you ever asked us out. We both thought we had a connection from the FNA. You are Rand, right, and you're friends with Ross? We have seen you two together a lot, but now that I think of it, we were never together when we saw you and Ross together." All Rand could get out was, "Whoa." He was stunned.

Finally, Rand got it together. "Wait here," he told Cindy. He then ran back to the pool tables. Before he got to the table where Ross and their friends were playing, Rand yelled, "Dude! They are identical twins." Rand accidentally hit Ralph's pool stick mid-stroke as he made his way over to Ross. Ralph turned around and shot Rand a look like he wanted to punch him in the face, but Rand was too excited and jumping up and down to notice. Partly because he was thrilled about the girls and partly because he needed to pee. "They are identical twins," Rand yelled again. "Who?" Ross said back. "Sandy and Cindy are identical twins," Rand explained.

Now Ross was jumping up and down. "Come on!" Rand yelled. They both ran back to where Cindy was standing and left their friends upset about the delay in their game of pool. Cindy was standing there and could not help but laugh at the two friends. Rand and Ross were running around like five-year-olds at a birthday party. Ross gazed into Cindy's eyes and was smitten all over again, but this time, it was okay to like her. There was a set of beautiful eyes for his friend as well. "You are Cindy?" Ross blurted out. Cindy replied, "Yes, I am Cindy."

Rand quickly asked, "Where is Sandy? Where is Sandy?" "She is over there in the bowling alley," Cindy explained. "We are kind of on a lunch date," she said. Rand and Ross glanced over and saw Sandy with her back to them but noticed the two guys sitting across from her. It was Russ and Mike. They had gone to Bonneville High School and played the same sports as them. They were rivals from the old high school days. Cindy, not wanting to stir up any trouble but wanting Sandy to hear the news, decided on a plan. She would try to wrap up the bowling activity with Russ and Mike as soon as possible and then bring Sandy over to where Rand and Ross were playing pool. Rand and Ross both agreed and said they would wait.

Rand finally made it to the restroom, and Ross explained as much as possible about what had just happened to their friends playing pool. Lyle asked, "Why didn't you guys tell us anything about these girls?" Ross exclaimed, "We thought it was the same girl! We didn't want to pursue her because of the other." Farrell chuckled and said, "You should have arm-wrestled for her." "Or a game of pool for her," Jody remarked. "A three-point contest," Ralph and Lyle said simultaneously. "It does not matter now. There is one for each of us," Rand said as he returned from the restroom.

The boys continued to play pool for about ten minutes when Ralph spotted two tall blonde girls walking towards them. "She is hot," Ralph said. "Both of them," Jody said. Rand was glad he used the restroom because he suddenly became so nervous he would have wet his pants if he had anything left or maybe something worse than just peeing. This was really happening, he thought.

Sandy and Cindy Simpson stood right next to each other, and they were two separate human beings. The only way the two boys could tell them apart was because Cindy was wearing a purple Weber State sweatshirt, and Sandy was wearing a red sweater. Both wore 501 jeans with the same Nike tennis shoes. They curled their long blonde hair very similarly. This was the eighties, so they both had big bangs and a lot of volume in their hair.

Sandy and Cindy began looking at Rand and Ross like, So what next, boys? Rand and Ross were almost trance-like. They had so many thoughts and emotions running through them that it took a moment to gain a train of thought. It probably did not help that Rand and Ross's four friends were hanging on every word spoken or, at this point, unspoken. Finally, Ross said to both girls, "We would love to spend some time with you two." Cindy decided to help them out. "Like a date?" she said. Rand blurted out, "Yeah, a date," as if he were a cat finally getting a furball out of his throat.

The many emotions that Rand had been feeling were now gone except for nervousness. Farrell could sense this and moved over behind him and whispered, "You are okay, Dude. Just relax." Luckily for Rand, Ross did most of the talking. "How about Friday night?" Sandy and

Cindy looked at each other and nodded with approval. Cindy found Ross's confidence appealing. Sandy thought Rand's nervousness was cute, at least for now. She could not help but hope that he would get over his nervousness soon, or it might be awkward.

Suddenly Rand blurted out, "I get so emotional baby. Every time I think of you." Everyone including Sandy and Cindy stared at Rand. The girls went on their way. Ross asked Rand, "What is up with the Whitney Houston lyrics out of the blue?" Rand answered, "I did not know what to say and it seemed like a good idea at the time."

Luckily for Rand, the nerves never lasted for too long. Rand had finally learned when he was nervous, to quit eating junk food and turn to comfort food. Mainly his mom's mashed potatoes and gravy. This would always ease his stomach. However, it seemed Rand had a new thing to combat his nervousness. Blurting out song lyrics.

Two nights later, it was Friday, and Rand was ready to go, and so was Ross. They had planned a fun and lively date. They picked the girls up at 5:00 in Bountiful, where they lived with their parents and two older brothers. They drove to Ogden to the Golden Spike Arena, where they went ice skating. Not knowing if the girls could skate was a bit of a risk. Sandy and Cindy could not only ice skate, but they were better than Rand and Ross. They were very coordinated, having danced most of their lives, and they had been on the drill team at Bountiful High School.

Now that the two couples had broken the ice (not literally), it was dinnertime. The group drove to Tony's Pizza in Ogden. Before the date, Rand had a steady supply of comfort food and felt well enough to venture into something risky like pepperoni pizza and soda. In fact,

Rand felt so good that he downed six slices of pepperoni and black olives by himself. However, this turned out to be a mistake.

The two couples had good conversations before, during, and after their meal. Rand and Ross explained how they had grown up together, all about their families and interests. Sandy and Cindy took turns explaining their lives and experiences. They both wanted to be dancers someday. "Where?" Ross asked. "Maybe New York City," Cindy answered. "Very interesting," Rand replied. The next stop was the Duck Pond at Weber State, but not before a slight detour.

Rand's stomach was giving him some issues after leaving Tony's. He had eaten too much pizza and drank too much soda. On the way over to the Duck Pond, it was stirring him up hard. Ross was driving his Honda Civic, and Rand and Sandy sat in the back. Ross was telling a story about their comeback victory over Bonneville their senior year. He turned to Rand in the back to see if he would join in on the story. Rand had the pale look on his face that Ross knew all too well. Suddenly, Ross had an idea. He turned back to Rand again and said, "Do you hear that noise?" Rand picked up quickly on what Ross was trying to do. "Yeah, I hear it," Rand agreed.

Ross pulled his car off to the side of the road on Harrison Boulevard. They both got out, moved to the back of the car, and acted as if they were trying to find the source of the noise, but there wasn't one. Rand thanked Ross for giving him an excuse to get out of the car. Then he broke wind much like he had done in the weight room back in high school. It was a good thing that it was not as rank as the experience in the weight room. Still, they stayed out of the car for a good five minutes to make sure the smell did not follow Rand back into the car. Ross acted as if he was giving his car a thorough inspection as Rand went about cutting the cheese.

Then they got back in the car and proceeded to the Duck Pond. Rand and Ross had told the girls to dress warmly, and it made sense to the girls when they went ice skating, but now, as they walked around the pond, it made even more sense to them. They wore thick coats, scarves, and gloves. It was a nice night out. It is a bit warmer than usual for early February but still a little chilly. On the way back, they stopped for some hot chocolate. The hot chocolate hit the spot in Rand's stomach.

Rand's stomach issues were the one glitch in the evening, and Rand and Ross felt like they had handled it very well. When they arrived at Sandy and Cindy's home in Bountiful, Rand and Ross walked the girls to the door. They had the usual end-of-date chit-chat, and then both girls turned to their dates at the same time and hugged them goodbye. As the men were walking away, Rand turned back and asked if the girls would like to go out the next weekend. Sandy and Cindy both smiled at the same time and said, "Sure." Sandy gave Rand their number, and Rand promised he would not forget it. Being a History major, Rand was good at remembering numbers and dates, so it was an easy promise.

Rand and Ross were on cloud nine. On the way back to the car, Ross turned to Rand and said, "Good first date." Rand replied with "yep" as he got into Ross's passenger seat. The talk on the way home to Hooper was a recap of the night's events. The girls seemed to enjoy the evening as well. Then, a thought occurred to Rand. He turned to Ross and said, "We walked both of them up to their door at the same time." Ross replied, "That would be awkward if we did not, right?" Rand then commented, "Well, it would be even more awkward if we were at the front door kissing them simultaneously." Ross laughed and said, "Dude, you are right. That would be awkward. We need to figure that one out in the future."

Chapter Four: Navigating Relationships

On the next date, Ross and Rand decided to stay in Davis County. They picked up the girls at 6:00 p.m. and drove to Kaysville. They dined at a local pizza restaurant. Rand learned his lesson last time and did not overindulge in pizza and soda. He was feeling much better after a good first date, anyway. After dinner, the foursome went to the Kaysville Theater and watched Caddyshack II. Ross and Rand loved comedies and assumed everyone else did, too.

Cindy and Sandy were hoping for a "chick flick" or something more serious, but they were happy to just be with Ross and Rand. During the movie, in a preplanned move, each girl reached out and held their date's hand. Ross and Rand could have been watching the biggest flop of all of time, and they wouldn't have cared. This was awesome, they both thought. They must really be into us to grab our hands. After the movie, they stopped for hot chocolate again and had more conversation.

Ross and Rand pulled up to the twins' house at the end of the date. They walked each sister up to the door again simultaneously, but this time, they paused to talk a little longer. It was Saturday, February 11, and Valentine's Day was just three days away. Ross asked the girls if they had any plans for Valentine's Day. Thankfully, both girls said no at the same time. Rand then looked at Sandy and asked, "Would you like to go out then? I know it is a school night, but we could get you back around 10:30 or so." Sandy smiled and said, "That would be great." Ross then nodded at Cindy and received the same grin back. Then, the girls reached out and hugged them, but this time, the hug was a little longer and stronger.

Ross and Rand drove home, and if there had been a cloud higher than nine, they would have been on it. The girls liked the boys. This was becoming obvious. Ross turned to Rand and said, "We have got to figure out the doorstep thing before Tuesday." "You are right," Rand said, "It is Valentine's Day, and the third date, which is the most common date to have a first kiss according to the dude on the radio, and they are clearly into us." Ross said as if he were dreaming, "Cindy has the softest hands." Rand could not help but laugh and said, "I think there is a tie for softest hands between Cindy and Sandy." They *were* identical twins, so they had to have equally soft hands.

They needed to figure out the end of the night kiss at the door. A completely different approach to the door that they had on their missions. Rand's truck did not seat four, so it required Ross to drive. Even the Civic was a bit of a tight squeeze. They contemplated driving separately, but if they were going to the same place, that would be weird and look as if they were up to something. However, they were up to something! They needed to figure out how to walk them up to the door at different times without looking too obvious. Besides, even if they drove separately, they would still arrive around the same time.

Rand said, "Maybe the girls will invite us in to meet their parents. Then we could try and stagger leaving." Ross shook his head and said, "We cannot guarantee they will invite us in. It is a school night, so they may need to get to bed or do homework. I think it is unlikely they will invite us in. Besides, what if they invite us in to meet their parents, and the parents linger after meeting us? We cannot kiss their daughters for the first time in front of them." "You are right," Rand agreed, "We can't ask their parents to leave so we can smooch with their daughters."

As the boys passed from Roy into Hooper, a thought popped into Ross's head. "How about when we arrive at their house, I tell Cindy I have a song I would like her to hear?" Rand quickly blurted out, "Okay, like from the Milli Vanilli cassette you just picked up?" Ross responded, "Everyone has heard Milli Vanilli dude, they are legit." Ross continued, "So, maybe that new Bon Jovi song that is starting to get big." Rand then yelled, "Yeah! Born to be my baby!"

"That is your cue then. When I bring up Bon Jovi, then you take Sandy to the door. When I see you coming back, that is when I walk Cindy to the door," Ross explained. "That is smooth criminal, dude," Rand said, referencing the Michael Jackson song. "Just do not be spying on us while you are waiting here in the car," Ross said. "I will be too busy with my own sweet memory," Rand responded.

Valentine's Day went according to plan. Ross and Rand took the girls to the Training Table Restaurant on Harrison Boulevard. Training Table was just down the road from Weber State. This was perfect because there was a Valentine's Day dance in the Sky Room in the Union Building at Weber State.

The two couples danced the night away. Ross and Rand believed they were really good dancers. They were athletic and listened to a lot of music. Cindy and Sandy were on a different level, though. They were great dancers, but it was a bit intimidating for Ross and Rand. They looked forward to the slow songs. The slow songs were less intimidating, and they could get close to their dates.

Once again, the two couples stopped for hot chocolate and then headed for Bountiful. The boys were both excited and nervous about getting back to Bountiful. Rand's stomach seemed to be holding it together nicely. Things were going so well that Rand did not see how this could go wrong. The doorstep went according to plan as well.

Ross stopped in front of the girl's home. He immediately told Cindy, "Hey, I have a new cassette you need to hear." Then, Rand got out of the car. Sandy paused because she thought they would all listen to Bon Jovi. Then she realized Rand was out of the car and inching toward the front porch. Sandy smiled when she realized what was going on. The boys were unaware that Cindy and Sandy were also trying to figure out how to be alone at the doorstep, but Ross and Rand had figured it out for them.

Rand and Sandy got to the doorstep. They turned and faced each other, both looking into the other's eyes. No words were spoken. This was a good thing for Rand. Sandy moved towards Rand like she had the two previous dates, but this time, she stopped before hugging him. Rand tilted his head and gently kissed Sandy goodnight. They separated after a few seconds. Sandy thanked Rand for the evening and wished him a happy Valentine's Day. Rand replied, "No, thank you! Happy Valentine's Day to you as well." Sandy turned and entered her house.

Rand walked back to the car. It felt like his feet did not touch the ground. Ross saw him coming and said to Cindy, "Enough of this song. Let's go in." Cindy smiled because she had figured out what was going on. Ross and Cindy walked up to the door as Rand slipped into the Civic. When Ross and Cindy arrived at the doorstep, they turned to face each other. Ross reached up and placed his hand on the side of Cindy's face and reached in and softly kissed her. Cindy told Ross, "Happy Valentine's Day," and then turned to her door. Ross replied, "Happy Valentine's Day," as Cindy walked through the door.

Ross then turned towards his car, punched the air, and said, "Sweet!" He got in the car, and the two guys high-fived each other. "What a night," Rand said, slowly accenting every word. "Best date ever," Ross said just as slowly, "Best night of my life." "Dude, no doubt," Rand commented. They both had warm memories of their twin for the ride home in the cold weather.

Chapter Five: The Next Step

Rand and Ross's next six months were a blur. By Spring Break, they were seeing Sandy and Cindy every day. The ladies joined Rand and Ross for lunch in the Union Building with the other dudes. Sandy visited Rand regularly at the Ogden City Mall. Ross worked full-time in the summer months for his uncle. So, Cindy would bring him lunch at least a couple of times a week.

Weekends meant the two couples were always together. They often went on regular dates, which meant dinners, movies, Weber State basketball games, and even the occasional Utah Jazz game. However, the two couples would rent a video occasionally and then just hang out and talk. They would also watch Utah Jazz games on television or even music videos on MTV at the twins' house. Life was good.

Rand and Ross bought playoff tickets for Game One of the Jazz series against the Golden State Warriors for Sandy and Cindy's twentieth birthday in April. The Jazz were upset, putting a downer on the night, but the boys took the ladies dancing at The Bay in Salt Lake City to salvage the night. The Fourth of July was spent in Hooper. There was a yearly celebration in Hooper, complete with an old-timer's baseball game, rides, a demolition derby, and fireworks to end the night.

After the fireworks, the two couples drove back to Bountiful. Sandy and Cindy suggested they walk over to a nearby park. The two couples split up at the park and walked in different directions. It was a beautiful night. Rand stopped walking, turned towards Sandy, and kissed her. Then, for the first time, he told her that he loved her. Sandy immediately replied, "I love you too." Then she kissed him back. Rand then held her in his arms. Life was good.

As Rand and Ross drove home, Rand thought about telling Ross that he had expressed his love for Sandy. It was not planned. He had gotten swept up in the moment, but Rand knew Sandy would tell Cindy. Then Cindy may wonder why Ross did not tell her that he loved her. She may even wonder if he loved her or if his feelings were not as strong for her as she felt for him. Rand did not want to cause trouble with Ross and Cindy. "I told Sandy that I loved her," Rand blurted out. "Dude! I told Cindy the same thing. I guess I got caught up in the moment," Ross said. "It was another great night, for sure, Rand commented, "It was easy to get caught up in the moment tonight." "Life is good," Ross said.

Rand and Ross could not believe how good their lives were now. They had turned twenty-two, and both had been home from their missions for about a year. Already, they were in love with wonderful ladies. Neither of them had planned on being in a serious relationship so soon after their missions, but that is exactly where they found themselves. Neither Rand nor Ross was going to complain, though. Life was good.

The next Sunday after the Fourth of July and the "I love you." Rand and Ross began to discuss their situation after church. Ross said, "The next step in the relationship will be getting engaged and then married." Rand nodded in agreement and said, "Do you think that is what the girls think as well? Are they ready for marriage? We are two years older and have lived in a foreign country for two years, and we feel sure that we are ready. But how do you think they feel?" Then Ross said, "Well, I guess there is only one way to find out."

That night, Rand and Ross continued to discuss where their relationships were headed. The men figured that if the twins did not feel the same way, then that would be okay. They would pump the breaks a little on their relationships. However, if the ladies felt like their relationships were headed towards marriage, then maybe they should start to make plans. Rand and Ross both agreed that they would talk to the girls together. The four were always together. It seemed perfectly normal to Rand and Ross to have a serious conversation with all four together. Besides, what affected one twin also affected the other.

Rand and Ross drove to Sandy and Cindy's house that evening. The four made their way downstairs to the basement after the men arrived. There was a TV room downstairs where the couple would often watch television or a video. The two couples sat on four chairs that were set up. Ross jumped in first, "We wanted to talk to you both about our relationships." Cindy replied nervously, "Okay." Ross continued, "We have been dating for nearly five months now. We were not expecting things to progress the way they have. Not that we are complaining. We wondered if you girls feel like our relationships were headed towards marriage. Should we slow things down, or are you both okay with the direction this is headed?" Rand nodded with approval as Ross talked, but the anxiety of the discussion finally got to him. "Cause it's a miracle. Oh, say you will, ooh babe. Hysteria when you're near," Rand sang during a pause in the conversation. The lyrics came from a Def Leppard song called Hysteria and from a very popular 80s album also called Hysteria. It seemed as though Sandy and Cindy were getting used to Rand blurting out song lyrics because they did not miss a beat this time.

Cindy replied, "We are glad you brought this up." Then Sandy chimed in, "Neither of us knew how to bring it up ourselves. We both feel we are in love. Though it has been unexpected how our relationships have progressed so rapidly, we like where things are going. If that means we are headed towards getting married, then that is more than okay with us." Rand quickly blurted out, "I like the sound of that."

Rand and Ross moved in for a kiss and a hug. Now that they all seemed on the same page, it was time for a plan. All four planned to return to Weber State for the Fall Quarter. If they took the Winter Quarter off to get married, work, and settle into married life, they could return to Weber State for the Spring Quarter of 1990. They all felt it was important to continue their education and not put it off. It would also be easier to get grants being married.

If they were going to get married in the winter, then when exactly? All four did not want to put it too far into January. They agreed to Friday, January 5th of the year 1990. There would be two Sealings on the same day. They would tell their parents but no one else. The twins' parents, of course, needed to know because they would be funding most of the wedding. Neither Sandy nor Cindy had a job. However, until it was an official engagement, they did not want anyone else to know—not even their siblings.

They all agreed that the Salt Lake Temple was where they would be sealed to their companion. They then started working backward on their timeline. The twins would take their endowments out on January 2nd in the Ogden Temple. Now, the two couples were set to get engaged. They would leave it like that for the time being. This had all happened so fast. Rand and Ross needed to purchase rings and to get officially engaged.

All four felt good about their wedding date. They had six months to prepare. On January 5th, it would have been about 11 months since they started dating and more than 13 months since they danced with each other at the FNA. Each relationship had progressed steadily and then really took off when summer came. Life was good.

Rand and Ross had both saved up enough money to purchase rings. The girls had given them some ideas about what they would like, so Rand and Ross went ring shopping. They purchased rings from the same store and around the same price, but unlike their soon-to-be fiancées, the rings were not identical. Rand purchased a triangular-shaped diamond, while Ross had bought a square-shaped diamond.

The 24th of July is a state holiday in Utah, which celebrates the arrival of the Mormon Pioneers in 1847. Both couples attended the Pioneer Days rodeo at Ogden Stadium on the 24th. The next day, Rand and Ross worked during the day but got off work early without telling the twins. They had asked the ladies to order pizza from a local pizza place and have it delivered. They would stop by their house that evening. Sandy and Cindy did as they were asked and ordered two pepperoni pizzas. They did not know that Rand and Ross had worked out a deal with the owners of the pizza place.

Rand and Ross had arranged for the pepperoni on the pizza to be placed into the shape of a heart instead of spreading out around the pizza. Next, they borrowed t-shirts and dressed as pizza delivery guys. Then, they arrived at Sandy and Cindy's, each carrying a pepperoni pizza with pepperoni arranged in a heart. Cindy answered the door and laughed at the sight of them. Sandy appeared as the boys made their way through the door. They then both got down on a knee, whipped out their rings, and placed them on top of the pizza boxes. Ross went first. On a bent knee, he looked up at Cindy and asked, "Cindy Simpson, will you marry me?" Cindy quickly responded, "Yes," and then got down on a knee as well and kissed Ross.

Now, it was Rand's turn. He was still down on a knee and looked up at Sandy, "Sandy Simpson, will you marry me?" Sandy also said yes, got down on a knee, and kissed Rand. With his seal of approval on the marriages, the girl's father, Jerry, was in on the secret pizza delivery. He had his camcorder out and recorded the entire thing.

The two couples were now officially engaged. They could announce their plans to everyone. The twins had already booked a date with the Salt Lake Temple for two back-to-back Sealings. Now it was time to figure out where the reception would be, order cakes, buy dresses, and order invitations. Jerry had set aside money, knowing the day would come when his daughters would get married. He thought it might be staggered a bit, though. He was not planning on a double wedding. "I guess I am paying for both games of a double-header," Jerry smiled and said to his wife.

Rand and Ross were smitten by Sandy and Cindy. They had a lot of fun with them. From a personality standpoint it seemed like both couples were perfect for each other. However, one big question neither Rand nor Ross asked themselves was just how spiritual the twins were. They were nice girls that attended Sacrament Meeting along with their other church meetings. Was this enough? How strong was their testimony of the Church of Jesus Christ of Latter-Day Saints? How would they respond if their testimony was ever tested? How would they respond when adversity affected their lives?

All couples will face adversity at some point. Who will they turn to when things get tough? Rand and Ross turned to their Heavenly Father and Savior Jesus Christ when they faced adversity in their life. Their parents had testimonies of the Church of Jesus Christ of Latter-Day Saints. However, Rand and Ross had developed their own testimonies. Would the twins turn to their Heavenly Father and Savior Jesus Christ during their darkest moments? Rand and Ross had not asked themselves these questions.

Up to this point, there had been no adversity in Rand and Ross's relationships with Sandy and Cindy. At least not since they figured out, they were identical twins and not the same person. The twins seemed to be smitten with Rand and Ross as well, but their relationships would soon be tested in an unforeseen way.

Chapter Six: The First Sign of Adversity

Both couple's relationships went very smoothly up to their engagements, and this continued after their engagements as well. As Summer ended and school started up, the two couples were back at Weber State for the Fall Quarter of 1989. Lunch in the Union Building, hanging out constantly, Utah Jazz games, and video nights continued through Fall.

Thanksgiving was spent at the Simpson home. The only downer was Ross and Rand's favorite football team, the Dallas Cowboys, were blown out by the Philadelphia Eagles. The twins' mother, Ann, made a fantastic Thanksgiving dinner, and her pumpkin pie for dessert was even better.

With a successful Fall Quarter at Weber State now over, the two engaged couples spent Christmas day together. They spent time at the Brooke, Fraser, and Simpson homes. Ross and Rand bought the girls beautiful CTR rings for Christmas. This was the second time the twins received rings from Ross and Rand that year. As the final minutes of Christmas Day 1989 ticked off, the two couples cuddled and dreamt of the many Christmases they would spend together. Life was good.

On New Year's Eve, the two couples went sledding on a hill by Roy High School. Ross and Rand created a large jump at the bottom of the hill by packing a bunch of snow in one area. Rand luckily wore his Dallas Cowboy helmet, which he received for Christmas when he was nine years old, the first time he tried the jump. After hitting the jump just right, he was thrown ten feet in the air and landed on his head. Even with the helmet on, Rand saw stars for a few minutes. Rand stood up was a bit wobbly. However, he was still able to get out some Madonna lyrics. "Crazy forrrr you," Rand sang and then smiled at Sandy.

After sledding, Cindy and Sandy went home to warm up with a shower. Ross and Rand did the same at their respective homes. The plan was to meet back around 8:00 in the Fraser's basement to bring in the new year. However, the twins did not arrive until after 10:00. Ross and Rand just chalked it up to women taking so much time getting ready. A thought that was a bit hypocritical of Rand since he was known for taking long showers and spending a lot of time getting ready.

Once the twins arrived, they all drank hot chocolate and conversed as they watched television. The conversation, though, was a bit different this time. Ross and Rand dominated the conversation but not by choice. It was due to the fact that Cindy and Sandy hardly said a word. This was unlike all the conversations the foursome had up to this point. They usually all participated in their conversations. This was why they got along so well. Rand loved Sandy, but he also got along well with Cindy. Ross and Sandy were the same.

Ross and Rand had always known each other, and obviously Cindy and Sandy had always known each other, but when they were all together, it was like all four had always known each other. However, as the eighties were coming to an end, this night was different. Neither Ross nor Rand had picked up on it, but something was wrong with the ladies.

Cindy and Sandy excused themselves to go to the restroom. It was not unusual if they were at a restaurant or ballgame, but it was unusual when they were at one of their homes. Ross and Rand continued their analysis of the Jazz season without noticing that anything was different. When the twins returned Sandy announced that they were not feeling well and were going to leave.

It was just past 11:00. Ross and Rand both stood up. "Are you okay?" Ross said. "We are fine," Cindy replied, "Maybe a cold or something, but we feel we should go home and get some rest rather than risk making things worse." "Yeah, okay. We hope you both feel better," Rand said. Rand and Ross walked the ladies to their car. Neither Cindy nor Sandy turned back to give their fiancée a kiss goodbye or even a hug. This would have been very odd had the twins not just told them they were feeling sick. Both men thought the girls didn't want them to catch what they had. "See you next year," Ross said, laughing. Ross and Rand watched as the girl's Jetta drove off. Little did they know that this was not just the last time they would see Cindy and Sandy Simpson in 1989, but for much longer.

Cindy and Sandy called the next day to cancel their New Year's Day plans. They had planned to eat Nachos, drink soda, and watch Bowl games all day. Since the twins were taking their endowments out on January 2, the next day, the men had thought they would take it easy on New Year's Day. "I guess we will see you tomorrow then," Rand said to Sandy when she called to say they were both still under the weather.

Ross and Rand retreated to the Brooke mancave downstairs in Rand's basement to watch college football. "They did not seem very sick, but I guess it makes sense not to take the chance of getting sicker with everything going on this week," Ross mentioned. "We are getting married in four days," Rand replied. "Yeah, we are, dude!" Ross exclaimed.

The plans for the week were all set. Jerry Simpson had told his daughters to have dual receptions at their Stake Center in Bountiful rather than an expensive reception center. They asked for the same Bridesmaids, so they did not need to buy extra dresses. Ross and Rand did not pay much attention to reception details or Bridesmaids' dresses.

Ross and Rand booked rooms at a hotel near the airport. They would spend their wedding night there and head out for Cabo San Lucas, Mexico, the following day. The members of Van Halen had a cantina there and spent a lot of time in Cabo San Lucas. The boys were hoping to run into them by chance. They were also excited to use Spanish, which they had rarely used since returning from their missions. Like many newlywed men, Ross and Rand would have preferred to skip the long reception and go right to the wedding night, but they knew that wouldn't happen because many girls started dreaming about their weddings and their receptions at the age of 5.

The next day, the twins had an appointment at 4:00 at the Ogden Temple to take out their endowments. Ross and Rand, their parents, and friends Ralph, Lyle, Jody, and Farrell would join them in the endowment session. The plan then was to head over to the Simpson home for refreshments. Cindy and Sandy were asked to arrive at 3:00 so they could be prepped for what would take place.

The Fraser and Brooke party arrived around 3:30. Ross checked in at the front desk to let them know they were with the Simpson group for the 4:00 session. Brother Fowers at the front desk looked at Ross strangely and said, "The Simpsons have not arrived, and I believe they have canceled their appointment." Rand quickly turned around, and as respectfully as he could, he told Brother Fowers, "There must be a mistake. We are marrying these two ladies in three days. I am sure they would have let us know if there was an issue." Brother Fowers replied, "I am sorry. You should contact the Simpson family. We do not have any more information than this."

<u>Chapter Seven: How Could Elvis Do This to Us?</u>

Rand and Ross each had a pit in their stomachs. Rand had suddenly wished he had not eaten at Taco Time for lunch. Ross looked at Rand, "They must still be feeling ill." Rand grabbed at his stomach, "Why would they not have called us though." Rand's mom, Lorna, said, "We should try and reach them before we jump to any conclusions." Ross thought this would be an excellent time to have one of those brick cellphone things that he had seen a few businessmen use while he mowed their lawns. Neither Rand nor Ross wanted to ask anyone at the Temple to use a phone. "We need to find a payphone," Ross's mom said. "Does anyone have a dime?" Ross's dad asked. "No, I think it costs a quarter now to call from a payphone," Rand's dad said. "Holy cow a quarter?" Ralph quickly blurted out, "I am not giving anyone a quarter to make a phone call."

The group turned back towards the front door to leave, with Rand and Ross leading. They saw Jerry Simpson walking around the fountain out front as they looked through the glass doors. "We will finally get some answers," Ross said.

Even though it was a cold, snowy day, Rand and Ross burst out the doors. They did not want anyone in the temple's foyer to hear their conversation with Jerry, but they also wanted to reach him as soon as possible. Jerry had a look of despair on his face. "I am sorry, guys. You do not deserve this," Jerry said softly.

"Where are the twins?" Ross asked. "Truthfully, guys, they are in Vegas," Jerry replied. "They need to take out their endowments if we are going to get married on Friday," Rand said weakly with the last bit of hope that this could still work out for them. "There is not going to be a wedding on Friday or any other day for that matter," Jerry said bluntly. "Someone got to them. We tried to talk them out of this. This is not what my wife and I want either. Again, I am sorry," Jerry continued. "Who got to them, Jerry?" Ross asked. "Look, the girls have made a tape explaining the whole situation," Jerry replied. "I have not listened to the tape. I hope they gave you the respect you boys both deserve. It should explain everything," Jerry said. Jerry handed Ross the tape, turned, and returned to his car. It was an awkward situation for him, and he would not stick around any longer than he needed to stay.

Everyone in the Brooke and Fraser group heard the entire conversation. A few were standing with their hands over their mouths in complete astonishment at what they had just heard. The others had placed their hand over their heart because they knew Rand and Ross were heartbroken. Rand and Ross turned around to their group without saying anything. Not even to each other. They then turned and started for Rand's truck. It had a tape deck, so at least they did not have to look for something to play the cassette tape on. The group followed them from a distance. They all wanted to know what was on that tape but knew Rand and Ross would have to listen to it on their own. Still, they wanted to be nearby to console them if needed, and it would be needed. Life was not so good.

Rand popped the cassette into the tape deck. He looked at Ross without saying a word but with an "okay, here we go" look on his face. Rand and Ross had learned to discern which voice was Sandy and which was Cindy in person. On a tape, though, it was impossible to figure out which one was speaking. One talked over the other a few times, so they knew they were both speaking on the tape.

Whichever twin was speaking, she got right to the point. "We asked our dad to give you this tape on the 2nd, so you do not have time to try and stop us," she said. "We just got off the phone to let you know we would not be coming over to watch any bowl games," she continued. "We have gone to Las Vegas with John Smith and Arnold George. We are marrying them tonight and will probably stay in Vegas for the rest of our lives," she said. "John Smith and Arnold George?" Ross asked. "We found a cute little chapel in Vegas with an Elvis impersonator that will marry us," she continued. "How could Elvis do this to us?" Rand asked.

Rand and Ross knew John and Arnold. They were friends who had played high school football with the twins' two older brothers. They were both very big guys, around 300 pounds each. After graduating from high school, they moved up to Bozeman, Montana, to play football for Montana State University. The previous summer, Rand and Ross had seen the two offensive linemen at the Simpson house a lot. They had supposed they were there visiting the twins' older brothers.

There were some things that Rand and Ross did not know about John and George. They had dated Sandy and Cindy during their Senior years of high school when the twins were Sophomores. When the two burly boys left for Montana, they bought promise rings for Sandy and Cindy. Jerry and Ann Simpson were unhappy about the rings, thinking their girls were too young for promise rings, and they were not particularly fond of either John or Arnold. They had heard rumors that both John and Arnold were womanizers, and Jerry and Ann Simpson did not want their daughters to be the next conquests of these two boys.

Every summer, when John and Arnold came home from Montana, they spent a lot of time at the Simpsons' home. They had no money to date, so they just hung out with the twins, watching cartoons. Jerry preferred them to be near so he could keep an eye on things. Then, this past summer, they expected to spend time with the twins again, but when they came home, Sandy and Cindy spent every day with Rand and Ross.

John and Arnold had exhausted their college eligibility and were home for good this time. Neither of them was close to graduating with a degree from Montana State after four years of school in Bozeman due to poor academic performance, but they hoped to get a job as bouncers at one of the clubs in Salt Lake City. They hoped to buy rings and ask the twins to marry them if they got jobs and if not maybe Sandy and Cindy could work and support them. However, they did not plan on Rand and Ross winning over the twins like they did.

John and Arnold had contemplated jumping Rand and Ross and beating them up. This was their way of dealing with competition. They had decided to go ahead with their plan in July when they heard the twins had agreed to marry Rand and Ross. They then worried that beating up Rand and Ross might bring the Hooper boys sympathy. They did their best to talk Sandy and Cindy into breaking up with the guys back in July. Then Sandy and Cindy could marry them instead, they reasoned. They had some friends they had played with in Montana who worked at a casino in Las Vegas. They could ditch Utah and all move to Vegas.

The twins wanted no part of that plan—at least not back in July. From that point, when John and Arnold came over to the house, they would tell them they could only stay if they were there to see their brothers. If they brought up Rand and Ross, they would have to leave. They were in love with those Hooper boys.

John and Arnold decided to make one last effort to convince the girls they were making a mistake on December 30. They figured if Sandy and Cindy kicked them out, the twins would get married and be gone soon anyway. John and Arnold started in on Rand and Ross by calling them the puny Hooper boys. They made fun of Hooper as a hick town. They made fun of Rand and Ross for going on missions and wasting two years of their lives. They had heard about Rand's flatulence issues and made fun of him. They made fun of them because they wanted to teach and coach. "You do not make any money in education. We will make the big bucks as bouncers in Vegas someday soon," Arnold said. John told the girls, "I thought you wanted to be dancers. We could get you jobs as dancers in one of the casinos." That seemed to hit the girls more than anything these two grizzly boys had said up to this point. Sandy and Cindy had always wanted to dance professionally. John and Arnold had gotten to the girls. Now that they would listen to them, they went in for the kill.

John and Arnold spent two hours that night telling Sandy and Cindy everything they thought was wrong with their future with Rand and Ross and everything they thought was right with a future with them. The girls went to bed that night, having doubts about Rand and Ross for the first time. They made the mistake of not getting down on their knees and asking their Heavenly Father for help. They just went to bed with the doubts in their head. The Holy Ghost was not with them to comfort them and let them know their plans with Rand and Ross were right.

When Sandy and Cindy said, "I love you too," to Rand and Ross back in July and later agreed to marry them, it was not a lie. They were both in love and looked forward to spending the rest of their lives with their Hooper boys. Rand and Ross had found a duplex in eastern Hooper. They planned to continue their education at Weber State after taking the Winter Quarter off. After graduating from Weber State, Rand and Ross still planned on teaching and coaching. Maybe they would end up coaching against each other someday and competing against each other like they did, crossing the corral with the bull in it as kids. It would be a lot of fun coaching with each other if it worked out that way. They told the twins that they hoped to have a dance studio at some point where Sandy and Cindy could teach different kinds of dance to kids and teenagers of all ages. The twins were enthusiastic about the lives that they had planned together with Rand and Ross.

Rand and Ross were different from any other boys that either of them had dated. They were spiritual. They prayed every day, read their scriptures, attended the Temple, and attended all their church meetings. More than anything, they were good people. They held doors open not just for them but for anyone. They served others. Rand and Ross visited the elderly in their ward and helped farmers around town.

Rand and Ross encouraged Sandy and Cindy to pray and read their scriptures. They discussed with Sandy and Cindy what they had been reading in the scriptures. The twins were the happiest they had ever been with Rand and Ross. For one vulnerable moment, John and Arnold had got to them. They had convinced Sandy and Cindy they could not be happy with Rand and Ross. They went to bed with doubts in their heads.

The next day, the doubts continued. They never picked up their scriptures or kneeled to pray. That day, they had fun sledding with Rand and Ross, as always. Then, when they went home to shower and got ready to go to Ross's house for New Year's Eve, the doubts came back. They were late arriving at Ross's house because they began discussing what to do. They had convinced each other to postpone their weddings until they could figure it all out.

They tried to get the courage to tell Rand and Ross that night. After arriving at Ross's house, they chickened out. They fled to the bathroom to come up with a new plan. They decided to make an excuse to leave and then find John and George. They were not only thinking of postponing the weddings, but they would also go all in on John and George's plan to move to Las Vegas.

The twins gave Rand and Ross the phony excuse they were sick. They left Ross's house and found John and George, who were where they had expected them to be, waiting at the Simpson residence. The twins arrived just before midnight. Just in time to give their new fiancée a New Year's kiss. Life was not so good for Rand and Ross. They just did not know it yet.

Chapter Eight: The Aftermath

Ross and Rand had been trying hard to keep it together, but this was too much. Tears began to flow out of both of their eyes. This was not a postponement or cold feet. This was a completely different course. They realized the girls were married the night before and had already spent the night with their new husbands. They were now Sandy Smith and Cindy George. Life was not so good. The group could see the tears and began discussing whether to move in to console them or wait for them to emerge from the truck. They decided to wait.

There was still much more to go on the tape, though. One of the twins asked if John and Arnold could buy the Cabo San Lucas package from them. She said that after they pay for the chapel and wedding in Vegas, they should have about $200 left. The other chimed in and said John and George were sure they could turn that into $1000 at the Blackjack table. They wanted to know if that would be enough to pay for the Cabo trip. It cut like a knife when one of the twins said their "new guys" did not like Van Halen, but they heard Cabo is a cool place, and they were willing to take the tickets off Ross and Rand's hands because they would not be honeymooning with them. Rand said with great astonishment in his voice, "What? Who does not like Van Halen? Everyone likes Van Halen." Ross added, "David Lee Roth or Sammy Hager, they are good either way."

Ross and Rand could not believe what they were hearing. It continued, "We do love the rings you guys bought us. We have decided to keep them. The guys would like to know how much they set you back. We already have jobs dancing in a show starting in a few weeks.

Arnold and John have jobs as bouncers in the same casino. We want to reimburse you for the rings," Ross said with amazement, "Are they serious?" Rand added, "The nightmare continues."

The nightmare would continue. The twins now twisted the knife and stated why they were not marrying them. None of it had ever been brought up before. "You guys are just too much alike," one of the twins said. "Wait, did identical twins just tell us we were too much alike?" Rand asked through sobs. "You have got to be kidding me," Ross added. She continued, "It was like we were dating the same person. You like the same movies, the same music, and you like the same teams." With his eyes staring at the tape deck like he was conversing with it, Ross just replied, "Wow." She continued, "We also know about Rand's stomach issues. We know that is why you pulled over on our first date. We didn't fall for the "did you hear that noise trick." Rand quickly replied, "I have not had any stomach issues since that night. How did they know?" Ross shot back and said, "Hey, this is not about your weak stomach, dude." Then Rand said whiningly, "I am going to have some issues tonight."

The words kept getting uglier from the twins. "We hate basketball," one of them said. "No, not basketball. That is a low blow," Ross said. "It is the greatest sport ever invented. Thank you, Dr. Naismith," Rand added. "Football is our sport," she said. "Since when, yesterday?" Ross said. "By the way, we are so sick of the Utah Jazz. We do not think Karl Malone and John Stockton ever have what it takes to get the Jazz in the NBA Finals. We also think Jerry Sloan is a terrible coach," she continued. "You are wrong about Jerry. He is a great coach. Tough as nails, too. He could take John and Arnold all by himself," Rand blurted out. "I could see Karl, John, and Jerry all making the Hall of Fame someday," Ross said.

The group standing close by could not hear what was on the tape but could make out some of what Ross and Rand were saying. After the comments about the Jazz stars and coach were made, the group began discussing the chances of the trio being in the Hall of Fame. All three were unanimously voted in by the group. "While we are talking about your favorite teams. The Cowboys are going nowhere fast. We do not see them winning a Super Bowl anytime soon. John and Arnold think the 49ers will be the team of the nineties," she said. "The Cowboys have only one way to go but up," Rand said. "Dude, they will be fine," Ross added.

The twins continued bashing Ross and Rand's favorite teams. "The Cincinnati Reds will never be more than a second-place team in their division. They will not be winning a World Series anytime soon," she said. "1990 is our year," Ross said. "You are right about that dude. Go, Reds!" Rand yelled. "Also, Weber State is not going to March Madness this year or any year. Let alone win a game in the NCAA Tournament like you guys think they will," she scoffed. "They are so cruel!" Ross exclaimed. "This hurts! I do not like the nineties. The nineties stink," Rand stated between sobs. "Yeah, the nineties stink. I miss the eighties already," Ross said, also between sobs.

The twins were still not done. "You are never going to go anywhere working in education. You are not going to make enough money. You both are going to be poor your entire lives. You make even less per hour as a coach than teaching. John and Arnold plan to bring in some big money in Vegas. They are going to make a difference," she said. "I do not care how much they are going to make; we will make a bigger difference as teachers and coaches," Ross quickly stated. "Without a doubt, dude," Rand said.

The twins then moved on to Ross and Rand's movie choices. "You know there are more movies out there than comedies. I mean, Caddyshack II for a first date, really?" she chuckled. "I thought it was a good show," Rand said. "It *was* a good show. The girls were laughing throughout the movie," Ross added. "Speaking of funny or not funny, have you guys ever noticed that you are the only ones who laugh at most of your jokes? You are not that funny," she added. "Let us know about buying the Cabo tickets and how much you want for the rings," she added.

The girls ended the nightmare by both saying, "Have a nice life." Ross and Rand wondered if the girls were being snarky when they told them to have a nice life. Either way, that is how it sounded to them. Life was not so good and now they knew it.

"Now what?" Ross asked. Rand cried, "Our entire lives were just turned upside down. I do not know where to begin. This hurts so bad." "How do we go on?" Ross asked. The two sat in the truck for a few minutes without saying anything. The group standing by was inching closer as they realized the tape was finished. Rand finally said, "We need to say something to our friends and family. I do not want to be rude to any of them, but I do not want to stick around for any pity party. I say we get right to the point to them with what the girls have done, and then we leave." Ross nodded in agreement.

Ross and Rand got out of the truck and stood before the group. It had just started to snow again, and the temperature was dropping fast. Rand started the announcement, "Cindy and Sandy went to Vegas yesterday with two other dudes." He paused briefly, then continued, "Elvis married them last night." The entire group gasped. "Elvis has not left the building" Lyle quipped. "They are going to be dancers in Vegas. They want to buy our honeymoon and rings and never see us again," Ross added. "Oh yeah, apparently they do not like basketball or anything else we like for that matter." Another gasp came from the group. "Who does not like basketball?" Lyle said. "Everyone likes basketball. That is a low blow," Farrell replied. "Salt in the wounds," Jody added.

Then there were a few moments of silence until Rand blurted out some Joan Jett and Blackhearts lyrics. "I hate myself for loving you. Can't break free from the things that you do. I wanna walk but I run back to you. That's why I hate myself for loving you," Rand sang. Everyone including Ross looked at Rand like he must be completely losing his marbles at this point.

"I say we go to Vegas and teach these two other dudes a good lesson," Ralph said. Lyle, Jody, and Farrell quickly agreed with Ralph. "The two of them are bigger than the four of you," Ross said, only slightly exaggerating. "Besides, that will not do us any good. It is over between us," Rand added. With those words, the tears came back to Rand's and Ross's eyes. The mothers of the two boys moved in to console them. Ross's mom asked, "What can we do?" Ross replied, "I think this is something we will have to figure out on our own." The rest of the group moved in and took turns giving Ross and Rand consoling hugs. After several more minutes of being consoled, Ross and Rand returned to the truck and drove off.

Ross and Rand decided to head to Burger Bar in Roy to grab a shake and a Big Ben. In high school, Burger Bar had always been a happy place for Ross and Rand. They had never taken Cindy and Sandy there, so it would not bring back any memories either. While they were eating, very little was said. After eating, they mutually decided to give the Cabo vacation to the girls as a wedding gift. Rand got a great deal from his friend Casey, who worked for a travel agency. So, the guys were not out too much.

The rings were a different story, though. Ross and Rand's savings had been nearly wiped out after purchasing the rings. The problem was how John and Arnold were going to come up with enough money to buy them. It was not like they could demand payment from John and Arnold or go to Vegas and take the rings back.

They decided to go to their homes and try to sleep. They would go to Bountiful in the morning to give the Cabo tickets to Jerry Simpson. Besides the honeymoon and rings, they had other things to worry about. They had put down a deposit and the first month's rent on their duplex. They had utilities that were set to be turned on. Cable television had finally made it to Hooper, and the cable guy was supposed to come between ten and two on Thursday. All this would have to be undone, along with canceling their tuxedos and hotel rooms for Friday night. Luckily for Ross and Rand, their families managed to contact every guest from their side who had received an invitation.

The next morning started at two in the afternoon for Ross and Rand. They had both tried to sleep but found it difficult. When they did sleep, it would be for about an hour, and then they would wake up thinking everything was a dream only to realize it was very real. Then, they would have a tough time falling asleep again.

Ross and Rand met at 2:30 and set out for one last drive to the Simpson home in Bountiful. Neither of them had showered, shaved, or eaten much, and they looked a bit disheveled. Life was not so good.

Jerry Simpson answered the door and looked pleased to see the two men. Ross and Rand told Jerry that they were giving the Cabo honeymoon to the girls as a wedding gift. Ann Simpson was in a back bedroom close enough to hear Ross and Rand. She could not compose herself enough to see them, but she wanted to be close enough to hear the men one last time. She was going to miss seeing them. She began crying again when she heard them say they were giving their honeymoon trip to her daughters as a wedding gift. She cried loud enough that Ross, Rand, and Jerry could hear her.

"That is incredibly nice of you guys," Jerry said. "Boys, I do want you both to know this is also really hard on us. We thought our daughters would be sealed to a couple of great guys. Now they are married to a couple of boys, we are quite worried about how they will be as husbands and eventually fathers to our grandkids," Jerry continued. "We are really sorry," Ross said. "We know we are not the only ones hurting right now," Rand added.

"Look, guys, I lost my deposit to the caterer, but I did save some money by not having a wedding reception this weekend. I would like to buy those wedding rings from you guys. I know the twins said they would keep and use them," Jerry said. "We kind of thought John and Arnold should come up with the money for those rings," Ross said. Jerry replied, "I think I have a better chance of getting reimbursed for those rings than you guys do now. Apparently, John and Arnold lost almost every cent playing Blackjack after their wedding. They are staying with some football buddies in Vegas. They are trying to scrape up enough money to drive back here to get their things. Now, they can come back, go to Cabo, and then grab their things before returning to Las Vegas. All four start new jobs in Vegas in a couple of weeks."

Jerry was right. They were not going to get a dime out of John and Arnold. Trying to get Cindy and Sandy to pay for the rings would not work out for them. Besides, neither Ross nor Rand wanted to communicate with Cindy and Sandy at the moment. They both wondered how long it would take for the twins to come up with the money for the rings. Ross and Rand both needed the money to get back on track. Besides, Jerry seemed to want to pay for them genuinely. They relented, and both took a check from Jerry for the rings.

"One last thing," Jerry said. "Those are some real nice CTR rings you got the girls for Christmas. They have left them here. I think they left them because they do not want to be reminded of what they have done, not just to you guys and us, but also from a spiritual sense. You guys should take them back. You could probably still get reimbursed for them," Jerry continued.

Ross and Rand took back the CTR rings. They each shook Jerry's hand, said goodbye, and headed for the door. Ann Simpson emerged from the back bedroom just before they reached the door. She was still crying, but not as hard as before. She gave both Ross and Rand a hug. She said nothing, nor did she need to say anything. The boys knew Jerry and Ann appreciated them. Ross and Rand shed a few tears, then said goodbye, turned, and walked out the door.

Everyone who knew Ross and Rand knew it would take them a while to get over Cindy and Sandy and return to being their usual selves. They were as fun, active, and successful as anyone. No one saw what would happen over the next year. Ross and Rand were neither fun, active, nor successful in 1990. Life was definitely not good for the Hooper boys.

Chapter Nine: The Nineties Suck!

No one would have blamed Rand and Ross for taking some time off from life. Their world had just been turned upside down in a very cruel way. Everyone who knew Rand and Ross hoped they would start feeling better in a month or two. People thought that maybe when they returned to work or attended a Friday Night Activity, things would start to feel better for them. Since the boys were taking the Winter Quarter off, some thought it might take until the Spring Quarter at Weber State that they start feeling better. No one guessed it would be an entire year for Rand and Ross to see the light of day, figuratively and literally.

Rand and Ross would rarely emerge from their rooms for days. They never shaved or cut their hair. They would go for several days without showering. Rand would not return phone calls to his boss at the Pro Image. It had been over a month, and every Pro Image employee had worked extra hours to cover for Rand, so the owners were forced to replace him. Ross was never officially let go by his uncle Brad, but Brad had lost one of his best workers. Not only did Ross work hard, but he could communicate with the Spanish-speaking employees for Brad. Brad also just missed being around his nephew.

Spring Quarter came, and neither Rand nor Ross registered for classes. Friday Night Activities were completely out of the question. Rand and Ross had met the twins at an FNA, and it would bring back too many bad memories. The boys never spoke the names of Sandy and Cindy. They never spoke about them, period.

Rand and Ross only left Hooper once a month. They would meet at Burger Bar. They could have a chance to make sure the other was doing okay, or at least okay in their eyes. They also talked about how long their hair and beards were getting.

They also met at the Hooper Store every day at 9:45, just before closing. They would buy what was left of the potato logs, mini-burritos, and chicken fingers that had not been bought during the day. They also each bought a six-pack of soda they would drink the next day. Besides the large amount of hair, they accumulated on their faces and heads, they were also gaining weight. Little activity combined with fried, starchy food and soda leads to weight gain. Whenever they met up, whether it was at Burger Bar or the Hooper Store, they always greeted each other the same way. One would say, "The nineties stink!" and the other would reply, "Yep, the nineties stink!" Life was not so good in the nineties.

The boys surfaced from their rooms a couple of times a day for meals they would take and eat in their rooms. Dirty dishes and empty soda cans would pile up in their rooms. Their families were trying to stay patient. They knew they were hurting, but they also knew they would not feel better until they returned to a more normal life.

Rand and Ross still had some entertainment in their rooms. Being a rural community, Hooper did not have cable television until 1988. In high school, Rand and Ross loved to hang out at friend's houses in Roy that had cable so they could watch music videos on MTV. This could be a friend of either sex. There was the occasional girl who thought Rand and Ross were at her house so much because one or maybe both were ready for a more serious relationship. This would cause hurt feelings when the girl would figure out the truth; Rand and Ross wanted their MTV. The girl would not stay mad at them for long. Rand and Ross were just too much fun to hang out with.

Now that Rand and Ross had cable in their homes, they could watch MTV all day, but this was the nineties, and they did not want to watch MTV in the nineties. The nineties stunk. They wanted eighties MTV; luckily, they had hours of recorded eighties MTV. In high school, Rand and Ross had two friends who did them a solid. Darin Jorgensen and Scott Grange lived in Roy and had cable television and, therefore, MTV. Rand and Ross bought dozens of blank VHS tapes, and Darin and Scott recorded hours and hours of MTV. Now Rand and Ross could escape reality and watch those VHS tapes for hours. In their eyes, it was a much simpler time. It was before that nasty cassette tape from the twins. It was before the nineties.

Besides letting themselves go physically, Rand and Ross also let themselves go spiritually. They did not pray or read their scriptures, and they did not even attend their church meetings. Rand and Ross were bitter and felt sorry for themselves. They were throwing their pity party. They also knew that feeling the Spirit would make them feel better, and they were not ready to feel better.

Rand and Ross's depressive state continued through Spring, Summer, and Fall, and their families were worried. The two families met often to try to come up with ways to get the boys out of their funk. They thought about getting them both some counseling, but how could they get them out of the house to see a counselor? Did counselors make house calls, they wondered?

Rand and Ross were bitter and mad at the world. On one particular night, when they met just before closing at the Hooper Store for leftovers and soda, they had a bit of a problem with some local farmers. During harvest season, farmers work late hours. They work early hours as well for that matter. Harvest season meant burning the candle at both ends for farmers. Most farmers would try to take a break in the late evening before continuing to work. These types of hours meant the farmers were not always in the best of moods when they stopped by the Hooper Store for a snack and drink before they jumped back on their tractors. On this October day, Rand and Ross pulled up to the store with their vehicles blaring rock music. Rand and Ross purchased their food and soda, and as they left the store, they could overhear a group of farmers chatting about their day while eating a snack. It was very common for farmers to take a break together at the store. One annoyed farmer yelled to Rand and Ross, saying, "Turn that racket music down long hairs." Rand responded quickly, "If it's too loud, you're too old." This was a common saying in the eighties, especially for those who listened to hair bands of the eighties like Rand and Ross.

Rand should have known better to cross a farmer during harvest season. He and Ross had seen plenty of fist fights between friends and even relatives over irrigation turns and stealing water. He quickly turned to see that this farmer was headed straight for him, and he was none too happy. His fellow farmers were right behind him. Rand realized he would not reach his truck before this group caught up to him. Luckily for Rand and Ross as well, Ross parked closer. Ross jumped in and yelled at Rand to get in. Rand grabbed the door handle on the passenger side, but it was locked. "Who locks their doors in Hooper?" Rand thought to himself. Ross did not have automatic locks, so he had to reach across and pull the knob on the passenger side to unlock it. The group of farmers was closing quickly. Rand finally opened the door and jumped into Ross's car.

The farmers were not quitting. They were very annoyed. "Get out of the car, long hair," the angriest farmer yelled. "Hey, isn't that Brother Widdison, our Elders Quorum President in our home ward?" Rand asked Ross. "Yeah, he probably does not recognize us," Ross replied. The other farmers joined in knocking on the windows of Ross's car. "Drive!" Rand yelled in a very panicked voice. Rand in a very upset voice started singing Sammy Hagar's I Can't Drive 55. Ross drove off and took Rand home. A couple of hours later, Ross took Rand back to the store to pick up his truck, hoping the coast was clear and his truck was unharmed. Luckily for Rand, both wishes were true.

The boys did not seem ready to talk to anyone. Though there was one person, they did open up to slightly. They both had a lot of respect for their Bishop, Dennis Moore. Bishop Moore would drop by several times a month to visit with Rand and Ross at their homes. Bishop Moore was brave enough to enter the boys' rancid rooms. Bishop Moore had a way of getting the boys to open up just a little bit without prying too much. The Bishop did not need to ask how they were emotionally or spiritually. This was obvious.

Bishop Moore would tell them some stories of his life and the obstacles he had growing up. The Bishop's parents had divorced when he was young, and he had also experienced a lot of heartache. When they talked about overcoming obstacles, they brought out the competitiveness of both Rand and Ross. Life is full of obstacles. They had never met an obstacle they had not overcome. However, this was a much bigger obstacle than they had ever endured. With each visit Bishop Moore spoke with them, he would start to see the light in Rand and Ross again. The Bishop would never lecture and even rarely spoke of spiritual matters. He did, nevertheless, have a calming influence on Rand and Ross. Rand and Ross began to feel more comfortable each time Bishop Moore visited. However, they never discussed the incident at the Hooper Store with Brother Widdison.

The family and friends of Rand and Ross thought they were dropping deeper and deeper into depression. Their appearance and smell were getting worse and worse for sure. Bishop Moore would update one of the parents as he left after a visit with Rand or Ross, and he would always have a different take than their parents. Bishop Moore would always say, "They will be fine. They just need a little bit more time."

There were a couple of ideas that would prove to be fruitful in helping Rand and Ross get over the hump. The first came from one of the get-togethers their families had to discuss Rand and Ross. The two boys regularly received letters from people from their respective missions in Venezuela and Argentina. The letters would come from members they had known in those countries and converts they had baptized. Neither Rand nor Ross would read the letters at this point in their lives. Each boy's mom discussed the letters at one meeting and decided to have them translated from Spanish to English so they would know what was written. They found some return missionaries in their ward who could speak, read, and write in Spanish to translate the letters.

The two moms loved reading the letters after they had been translated. The letters were mainly updates from members to let them know what they had been up to back in their own countries. The major theme of the letters was how school was going for their kids, what sports their kids were playing, and any trips they may have gone on. The moms asked the same Spanish-speaking return missionaries in their ward to return the letters, let the people know about the circumstances of their sons, and ask if they would write them something inspirational with their testimonies.

The letters were written during the Thanksgiving break and sent to Venezuela and Argentina. The families were worried that this Christmas holiday season might send Rand and Ross into a deeper funk. One year ago, they were preparing to marry Sandy and Cindy in the Temple, and they were now approaching the anniversary of the breakup.

Every letter sent to Venezuela and Argentina was returned before Christmas. The two moms planned on trying to read the letters to their sons on Christmas morning. Rand's mom walked down the stairs to his smelly room. "I want you to do one thing for me," she said. Thinking she wanted him to shower or shave, Rand replied, "Not today, Mom." His mom pleaded, "It is Christmas. Would you please listen as I read something to you?" Rand was taken aback. "It is Christmas," he said. "Yes, and I have some letters from Argentina, I want you to hear," she said. "Do you speak Spanish now, Mom?" Rand replied, not knowing the letters had been translated already.

Lorna ignored the last comment and began to read the letters. Letter after letter spoke of how Rand had influenced them in some way. More specifically, Rand had the Spirit with him in everything he did as a missionary, and he also helped others feel the Spirit. Each letter had a testimony from every person who wrote it. Some families had sent letters from each member of their family. The children seemed to get to Rand.

When Lorna finished, Rand told her, "Thank you, Mom. This is the perfect present for me." Lorna decided to leave the room and leave Rand with his thoughts. As she left his room, Lorna looked back and said to Rand, "I love you, son." Rand replied, "I love you too, Mom."

Lorraine entered Ross's room and asked if she could read him something. "I am tired. I just want to sleep." Ross replied. Lorraine asked, "Will you please listen to these letters? They are from Venezuela." This got Ross to roll over. Lorraine did not hesitate. She began reading the letters. Like Rand's letters, the letters from Venezuela also discussed Ross's influence. Brother Concepcion said Ross had the Light of Christ with him. Each of Ross's letters also bore of Christ as the Savior, Heavenly Father has a plan for each of us, and there is a Prophet on the earth today. Lorraine finished the last letter with tears in her eyes. She got up and turned to walk out of Ross's room. Ross had not said one word as his mom read the letters. "I love you, Mom," Ross said just before Lorraine walked out of the door. Lorraine looked back and said, "I love you too, son."

The letters had a definite effect on both Rand and Ross. They both showered that day. They even left their rooms and walked around their houses. They wished everyone in their family a Merry Christmas. The letters helped them realize that the love they had lost did not take away from the love they already had. Many people in this world loved them, and they loved them too.

The second idea to help Rand and Ross came from Ross's Uncle Brad. The landscaping business was doing well. Brad had purchased an old building kitty corner from the Hooper Store and across the street from Hooper Elementary. Brad had thought he would store some of his landscaping equipment in the building. Then he came up with the idea of doing some extensive remodeling to the building and make it into a restaurant. He knew nothing about owning a restaurant, and neither did Rand and Ross, but he thought putting them in charge of this restaurant might get them back on track. It was a risk Brad was willing to take.

Putting a restaurant in Hooper was literally a risky business. The four-way stop where the restaurant would be located is considered downtown Hooper if there was such a thing. Next to the Hooper Store was the Hooper Post Office. On the other side of the school was Boheme's Garage. That was it. The other issue is that Hooper is not on the way to anywhere. To get people to drive to Hooper, the restaurant would have to be worth the trip.

Brad called both boys the day after Christmas and told them he had someplace he wanted them to see the next day on the 27th. Rand and Ross agreed to go. It was certain that they would have found an excuse not to go had Brad asked before Christmas. The letters had softened the two, but not enough to get a haircut or shave. After nearly a year without cutting their hair or shaving, they looked like Grizzly Adams, the main character in a television show by the same name from the late seventies and early eighties.

Brad picked them up and drove them to his "new" old building. When Rand got in Brad's truck, he immediately said, "The nineties stink!" to Ross, who was already in the truck. Ross returned a "The nineties stink!" back to Rand. "Speaking of stinking, I want to thank you both for showering this morning," Brad said dryly. This got a laugh out of Rand and Ross. Brad was happy he would not have to use the can of Lysol or car fresheners he had just purchased for the occasion after all.

The building had seen better days, so it was difficult for Rand and Ross to imagine this being a restaurant. The wood foundation was rotting, and the place had not seen any paint in decades. Brad sensed their skepticism, "We would probably have to tear it all down and rebuild it, but I know people that could help us with that," Brad said. "Us?" Ross replied. "Yes, I want you two to run this place. You can design it, develop a theme, hire a staff, the whole nine yards," Brad said.

Rand and Ross looked at each other. Neither said anything for a couple of minutes. They just looked at the building and then looked at each other. Brad decided not to say anything and let their minds go. Finally, Ross said, "What if we turned it into an eighties place?" Rand smiled, "Yeah, the nineties stink!" Ross fired back, "Yep, the nineties stink!"

Brad was skeptical, "The eighties ended less than a year ago. In 25- or 30 years, people may be nostalgic about the eighties, but not now." Ross quickly replied, "Yes, but the eighties started eleven years ago." The creative motors in both Rand and Ross were churning for the first time in almost a year. "We could have an arcade on one side with eighties video games like Frogger, Asteroids, Galaga, Space Invaders, Pole Position, Centipede, and Mario Brothers," Rand said. "You could probably pull a profit with the quarters in the arcade alone," Ross agreed. "Okay, I would probably have a few people upset with me for putting an arcade across the street from an elementary school, but I like where this is headed," Brad said. "How about booth seats for the restaurant, and each booth would have a mini jukebox with only eighties songs in it?" Ross continued. "How about we mount some televisions, and we could play eighties movies and even eighties MTV from all the tapes we have," Rand added. "Also," Ross cut in, "we could have posters of eighties bands and musicians along with some eighties movies." This got Rand excited, "Yes!" he said. "I know, each menu item could be named after an eighties artist like Cindi Lauper fries, Bon Jovi shakes, and the Bono burger. We could also have theme nights celebrating events, movies, television shows, and bands from the eighties," Rand added. As the three men drove off, it was very clear that Brad's plan to give them something to be excited about was a success.

Rand started singing on the way home. "I love rock 'n roll, so put another dime in the juke box baby. I love rock 'n roll. So come and take your time and dance with me. Owww!" Rand sang. Rand's disposition had changed a great deal as he sang another Joan Jett and the Blackhearts song. Ross was upbeat as well as he began to sing a song by Mr. Mister. "So, take these broken wings and learn to fly again. Learn to live so free," Ross sang.

Chapter Ten: The 80s Guys

Ross and Rand met on New Year's Day to set some goals. They felt better about life but were not completely out of their funk yet. The timing of the restaurant could not have been better. It had been over a year, by a few hours since they had seen Cindy or Sandy. They needed this diversion.

The first goal on each of their lists was to take a shower each day. Everyone in their lives would be excited about this goal. The next goal was to create, along with Brad, the coolest restaurant in the entire state of Utah. The third goal was to lose the 25 or 30 extra pounds they were now packing. These were the only goals they listed. They did not set goals for reading scriptures, attending church, or saying their prayers every day.

Besides the goals, they also made two pacts with each other. The first pact was to shave off their scraggly beards. They were going to keep their long hair but get rid of their beards. The other pact was to swear off not only the nineties but any decade other than the eighties. They would dress, talk, and act like they were still in the eighties.

Ross and Rand had isolated themselves so much in the past year that they had missed out on all the events of 1990. They did not even follow sports for that year, so they missed out on their favorite baseball team, the Cincinnati Reds, winning the World Series by sweeping the Oakland A's. This was the first of the predictions Cindy and Sandy made about their sports teams that did not come true. The Reds won the World Series in 1990, the Dallas Cowboys won three Super Bowls and were considered the team of the nineties, the Jazz led by future Hall of Fame Coach Jerry Sloan and fellow future Hall of Famers John Stockton and Karl Malone, did make the Finals in 1997 and 1998, and Weber State went to the NCAA Tournament in both 1995 and 1999 and won a game in the tournament each of those years.

Ross and Rand's devotion to the eighties would go hand in hand with the restaurant they would soon run together. Brad went to work on the restaurant's construction while the men worked on ideas to accomplish their goal of having the coolest restaurant in the entire state. The three men hoped to get the restaurant up and running by early June, so the opening would coincide with the end of school.

As Winter turned into Spring, Ross and Rand felt and looked better. Their attitude was still not great, but better. They got out of bed and showered every day. They still had not cut their hair, but they shaved semi-regularly. They were not back in school, but they worked on the restaurant every day.

The biggest concern for their families was that they still did not go to church or do anything spiritual. They were not dating, nor did they try to date. They were still hurting inside, and both men were trying to figure it out. They were not ready to return to their old life because they were still not themselves.

Bishop Moore continued to visit them regularly, making it a point to check on one of them every Sunday. Ross and Rand looked forward to the visits from Bishop Moore. They always felt better about themselves after talking with their Bishop. Bishop Moore continued to preach patience to Ross and Rand's parents.

During the second month of construction, Ross and Rand went to Brad and asked for an addition to the restaurant. They wanted a room and bathroom in the back of the restaurant. Ross and Rand wished to live at the restaurant. Brad worried that Ross and Rand's idea was a method to cut off the outside world even more. The two men rationalized living at the restaurant as a convenient way to be around for deliveries during odd hours and that there would be no need for security with them there overnight. "Since when was security needed in Hooper?" Brad asked.

Ross and Rand were fine living at home. They appreciated how much their parents had helped them through a tough time. They would be 24 years old soon and had been home from their missions for almost three years. They were ready to be out on their own, even if that meant living in a back room in their restaurant.

Brad talked it over with Ross and Rand's parents. Brad was surprised that they all liked the idea. All four felt it would help the healing process for Ross and Rand to get out of their parent's home. Besides, it was not like they were going extremely far. They would still be in Hooper. Even with Rand's home on the last road in Hooper, it was still just two miles away. It seemed like a good situation, so a room and bathroom were added to the blueprints.

In April, Brad surprised Ross and Rand when a giant neon electric sign arrived. The sign would be assembled to the front of the restaurant and state the new name. A truck delivered the sign covered with a tarp. Brad came by just in time to unveil the sign to Ross and Rand. The sign read in orange and yellow cursive, "80s Guys," and below it in smaller block letters, "Restaurant and Arcade." Now, the restaurant had a name.

Ross and Rand had discussed names for the restaurant but could never agree. Then, one day, Brad said he would take care of it. The men did not argue since it was Brad's money going into the restaurant. He was the one taking the risk. Brad ordered the sign without telling Ross and Rand what he had decided. Now that the sign had arrived, the two men loved the name, and they loved the sign.

As the 1991 calendar moved into May, the restaurant's finishing touches were taking shape. The booths were all in, as were the mini-juke boxes in each booth. Posters were hung of great eighties music groups, including Bon Jovi, U2, Journey, Def Leppard, Van Halen, Madonna, and Michael Jackson. Posters of eighties movies, such as Better Off Dead, Pretty in Pink, and Ferris Bueller's Day Off, were also included. Televisions were mounted and wired into VCRs that would play eighties movies and music videos from the eighties.

Ross and Rand began to hire a staff. The two men had decided the staff uniform would consist of 501 jeans, white sneakers, and a t-shirt or sweatshirt from the eighties, depending on the season. Most of the staff hired were big concertgoers with a good supply of concert t-shirts from the eighties. There were also staff members with shirts from eighties sport team championships and eighties movies. Everything was coming together for the big opening on Friday, June 7th. School would be out for the summer, and Ross and Rand advertised it in local newspapers and on the radio. They just knew the restaurant was going to be a hit that summer. The key would be sustaining success after the hoopla had worn off.

The 80s Guys Restaurant and Arcade was officially completed on the last day of May, and the building received the go-head with a certificate of occupancy. There was now just one week before opening. Ross and Rand were hard at work training the staff and getting the last deliveries before the opening. The two men had done their research on running a restaurant by visiting and speaking with several local restaurants. They both felt ready. Now, they just needed for June 7th to arrive.

When the day finally arrived, the ribbon-cutting ceremony was at ten o'clock that morning, and Brad was doing the honors. Most of Hooper showed up. After the ribbon was cut, dozens of elementary and junior high-aged kids entered the arcade and started pumping quarters into the video games. The restaurant also filled up fast for those wanting an early lunch. A waiting list was immediately set up, and customers were nonstop throughout the day. 80s Guys stayed open until midnight on the first day, and the restaurant was full until ten minutes before closing.

Ross and Rand quickly went to work cleaning the restaurant, bathrooms and all, after closing. They would serve as custodians until the financial outlook of the restaurant became clearer. After they finished cleaning, it was around two in the morning, and the 80s guys retreated to their room. They had moved in the previous weekend when the building was completed. "We did it, dude," Ross said as he lay on his bed. "We sure did," Rand replied as he collapsed on his bed. Within seconds, the two were fast asleep.

Ross and Rand were back at it early the next day. Saturday was just as busy, with constant customers in the arcade and restaurant. Those who did not get a chance to sit down and eat on Friday were there on Saturday. Word was getting around as more customers outside Hooper came to eat on Saturday. The 80s guys again retreated to their room early in the morning after everything was clean. After two very busy days, they would have a chance to rest on Sunday when they were closed.

Ross and Rand knew the restaurant could not keep up the pace it set on the first two days. Still, the arcade and restaurant were busy throughout the summer of 1991. Families loved coming to 80s Guys. The kids would spend a dollar or two in the arcade while they waited for their meal. The parents would put a few dollars in the jukebox at their booth while they waited to be served. The restaurant was also great for a guy to take a girl on a date. The food was great, especially the Bono Burger and Bon Jovi shakes. The music and movies of the eighties were also great icebreakers for a date. The booths were filled with discussions on favorite movies, songs, and music videos from the eighties. Married couples also found 80s Guys a great place for a date night. Kids riding home on their bikes after baseball or softball practice would stop into 80s Guys to buy a soda and play some video games. Those of all ages found 80s Guys a great way to spend an evening. Business was booming.

As school started back up for kindergarten through twelfth grade in late August, Ross and Rand knew business would slow down at 80s Guys. They would also take a smaller hit when Weber State, now a university as of January 1st of 1991, returned for Fall Quarter. Business did slow down, but not as much as they expected. The 80s Guys became a popular business lunch destination. After a good month, bosses rewarded their employees with lunch at 80s Guys. Parents who wanted to take a night off from cooking would take their families to 80s Guys for a dine-out evening. When the holidays came, 80s Guys had Christmas parties nearly every night in December.

Business continued to thrive into 1992. Ross and Rand were working hard and loving every minute of it. Their confidence was back, and they enjoyed themselves. Still, something was missing in their lives.

Chapter Eleven: A Good Place

In the Fall of 1991, the Hooper Stake started a single adult Branch. Many of Rand and Ross's friends attended the Branch. Ralph, Lyle, Jody, and Farrell were now married. The four and their wives were regulars at 80s Guys. The Branch consisted of many friends from high school and the Hooper Third Ward, where Rand and Ross grew up.

Bishop Moore still visited Rand and Ross regularly, but he could now visit both at the restaurant. Bishop Moore told them about the new single adult Branch. He never put any pressure on them to attend but wanted them to be aware that it existed. Friends who attended the Branch were regulars at 80s Guys and made sure Rand and Ross knew about the weekly Monday activity and other fun experiences going on in the Branch.

Sundays were a day of rest for Rand and Ross. The restaurant was busy, and they were involved in all aspects of the restaurant from cooking to cleaning to playing movies or music videos on the televisions. They also made sure every customer was happy and joined in on any eighties conversations and analyses that were brought up. When Sunday came, they were tired and needed that day of rest.

Rand and Ross's Sunday conversations revolved around how blessed they were. Sandy and Cindy never came up directly. Indirectly, they were only brought up as something they had been through or a tough period in their lives. They had sworn off the nineties because they were bitter about what Sandy and Cindy had done to them. The restaurant had helped them overcome the darkness that came after the twins. They were ignoring the nineties, not out of bitterness, but because the eighties, through the restaurant, brought them joy again. Their turnaround was not yet complete, however.

On a Sunday in mid-March, Rand and Ross were resting at 80s Guys and conversing about how blessed they were. "Dude, what do you think about the singles Branch?" Rand asked. Ross was blunt in his response. "I think we need to go back to church, and I think we need to think about getting back into the dating scene again. The singles Branch could do both for us," Ross said. "Yeah, I agree," Rand commented.

Just then, there was a knock on the back door. It was Bishop Moore. "Have you hidden a microphone in our room?" Rand asked after letting the Bishop inside. The three men walked up to the front of the restaurant and sat down at one of the booths. "Why do you ask about a microphone?" Bishop asked, still chuckling at Rand's question. "We were just talking about the Single Adult Branch as you knocked," Rand replied. "We are thinking about attending," Ross added.

The Bishop smiled at the two 80s guys. Rand continued, "We both feel good about our lives, especially after everything we have been through. There is still something missing, though." This is what Bishop Moore had been waiting and praying to hear. "As much as I would love having you back at the Hooper Third Ward, I think the singles Branch would be a good thing for you guys right now," the Bishop said. "We need to feel the Spirit again. We need to take the Sacrament," Ross added.

Bishop Moore's eyes began to glisten. He knew Rand and Ross would come around. He had told their parents to be patient. Bishop Moore knew Rand and Ross had a testimony. They just needed to deal with their heartache in their own way. The Spirit was in the room, and the Bishop felt he should be more direct with Rand and Ross.

"I am going to ask you guys some difficult questions," Bishop Moore said. "I think we need to get some things out in the open," Ross replied. "I think we are both comfortable talking about what happened with the twins with you, Bishop. That is what you were meaning about difficult questions, right?" Rand added. "Yes," Bishop Moore quickly agreed.

Rand and Ross both took a big breath. "Why did the twins do what they did?" Bishop Moore asked. This was a question both Rand and Ross had thought a lot about since January 2, 1990, now over two years ago. Even though both had thought about what happened with Sandy and Cindy, neither had spoken about it. Not even with each other. "I think they were easily swayed by two selfish guys because they did not have the Spirit with them," Ross said. "I agree. Looking back, I realize they did not have a personal testimony of the Savior and that he is the head of our church," Rand added.

There was a ten-second silence as Rand and Ross thought more deeply about what they had just said. Then Rand continued where he left off, "They grew up different than we did. There is not much that they have had to work for in their lives. They have never had a job before. Their parents paid for college, their car, and anything they needed. Because of this, they did whatever their parents said they should do. They went to church because their parents told them they should. They went to college because their parents told them they should. They probably dated us because their parents liked us. The one thing they worked hard at was dancing, and they loved it." Ross now jumped in, "We probably did not realize how much they enjoyed dancing. I agree that is the one thing they had to work for in their life. They are dancing now, I guess."

There was another pause in their discussion. Then Ross continued his thought, "As hard as that was to get through, I am glad it happened. We probably would have been okay being married to them, but what if we had something difficult to get through in our marriage? Financial issues, health issues with one of our children, or a disagreement. Would they have bailed on us when things got tough? Would they have returned to Mom and Dad for help, or would they have tried to work it out with us? I want to be married to someone who has a personal testimony of the church and our Savior. I want to be married to someone that I know no matter how hard things get, we will be okay. We can overcome any obstacles in our way." Rand quickly added, "I could not agree more. They are not bad girls, but they made a bad decision. When those guys got to them, they did not ask Heavenly Father for help. That was why they were so easily swayed."

Bishop Moore nodded in agreement with every word out of the mouths of Rand and Ross. "I am glad to hear that, you guys. I never questioned your testimonies." Bishop Moore said. Rand replied, " My biggest regret is that we stopped doing things we have done our entire lives, like reading the scriptures, praying, and going to church. We would have recovered quicker had we been doing those things, but we laid around feeling sorry for ourselves. In a way, we did what the twins did. We did not turn to our Heavenly Father to help us." "I agree. We should have done better doing those things all along. I have missed feeling the Spirit," Ross added.

The Bishop left that night knowing Rand and Ross were in a good place. Rand and Ross also knew they were in a good place. They had overcome the emotional trauma that followed their breakup with the twins. Now, it was time to get back on track in a Spiritual sense. They had not been doing the things to bring the Spirit into their lives. At least they had no bad habits or serious sins to overcome. They still had long hair and listened to music really loud. One of their favorite sayings was still, "If it is too loud, you are too old." They both knew they needed to go back to church and take the Sacrament regularly.

Chapter Twelve: Progressing

The following Sunday, Ross and Rand attended church at the Hooper Single Adult Branch. Most of the Branch were single adults from Hooper. Everyone from Hooper knew the 80s guys, and their restaurant. Those who attended the Branch who came from Roy, West Haven, Taylor, Sunset, West Point, Syracuse or just about anywhere in Weber and northern Davis County knew the 80s guys.

When Ross and Rand walked into the chapel about five minutes before Sacrament Meeting started, it felt like every eye was on them. Maybe because every eye in the chapel WAS on them. Ross and Rand walked up to the second pew on the left side of the chapel. "I feel like every eye is on us," Rand said. "Everyone is looking at us," Ross replied. "Is it because of the long hair?" Rand asked. "Maybe," Ross said. "Is it because we are new?" Rand asked. "Maybe," Ross replied. "Is it because everyone knows the 80s guys?" Rand asked. "Maybe," Ross said. "Maybe it is because the girls think we are cute," Rand said. "Maybe, well, that is obvious," Ross replied with a smile and then continued as he scoped out the chapel, "That would not explain why all the guys are looking at us as well, though."

As the meeting started, Ross and Rand forgot about any eyes that may be on them. The Spirit was strong in this Branch. Ross and Rand felt the Spirit not just in Sacrament Meeting but also in Sunday School and Elders Quorum. After church, some women approached Ross and Rand and invited them to an unofficial Branch activity. Ross and Rand soon learned the Branch had an unofficial activity every Sunday and an official activity every Monday. The Sunday activity was at one of the Branch member's houses, and they would play games, socialize, and hang out. The Monday activity was Family Home Evening with the Branch family. These activities could be more Spiritual, like a group discussion on a Spiritual topic or a speaker from outside the Branch. There were also times when the Monday activity was a game or activity that was less serious.

Ross and Rand enjoyed the Sunday and Monday activities. They quickly got to know everyone in the Branch. The Branch was not cliquish. Everyone seemed to get along with everyone else. Ross and Rand were impressed with how much time and effort those who spoke in Sacrament Meeting and those who gave lessons put into their talks and lessons. Michael Moulding, the Gospel Doctrine Teacher, was able to get everyone involved in the discussion of each Sunday.

After the fourth week of attending the Branch, Ross and Rand came to a decision. "I think it is time to cut our hair," Ross said after returning from church. "Yeah, I think you are right, dude," Rand agreed. Their long hair was great for theme nights at the restaurant, involving the hair bands of the eighties, but not cutting their hair became a symbol of not moving on from the twins. They both felt they had moved on, and it was time to cut their hair. The next morning, they went in to see Brenda, a friend from high school, and she cut their hair for the first time in almost two and a half years.

Ross and Rand were feeling the Spirit again—not just on Sunday. They both read their scriptures daily again. They also attended the Temple every Tuesday morning before the restaurant opened. Life was good again—really good.

Ross and Rand both had favorite scriptures that touched them in the most difficult times. For Ross it was Alma 62:41, which reads:

But behold, because of the exceedingly great length of the war between the

Nephites and the Lamanites many had become hardened, because of the

exceedingly great length of the war; and many were softened because of their

afflictions, insomuch that they did humble themselves before God, even in the

depth of humility.

While Ross had not been through war he had been through a traumatic experience. He

had become hardened to the Spirit. Once Ross was able to humble himself, he was better able

to deal with those afflictions that he had experienced. The Spirit was once again in his life and

the darkness that he felt had passed. He was more like himself again.

Rand loved the scripture found in Ether 12:27. It reads:

And if men come unto me I will show unto them their weakness. I give unto men

weakness that they may be humble; and my grace is sufficient for all men that

humble themselves before me; for if they humble themselves before me, and

have faith in me, then will I make weak things become strong unto them.

Rand realized he had learned so much from the trials he had recently experienced. Ether

12:27 showed Rand that he could take these trials that had weakened and humbled him and

used these experiences to strengthen himself. His testimony had grown, and he would never

take the Gospel of Jesus Christ for granted again.

Ross and Rand also began to date again. Not any serious dating. They would each ask a member from the Branch and then flip-flop a couple of weeks later, with Ross asking out the women Rand had been out with and vice versa, much like they had in high school. With all the changes in their life, neither Ross nor Rand was quite ready for a meaningful relationship.

June rolled around, and 80s Guys had a big celebration for their first anniversary. Every item on the menu was half off if you came dressed as your favorite eighties actor or musician. One red-haired woman was a dead ringer for Tiffany, who famously sang "I Think We're Alone Now." The music video was shot at the Ogden City Mall. Ross and Rand had some friends you could see in the music video that played regularly on MTV in 1987.

Ross and Rand made another big change in their lives in the summer of 92. They decided to go back to Weber State and finish their degrees. The 80s Guys Restaurant was doing so well that they could hire a friend, Diamond Dave Paulsen, to open the arcade and restaurant in the morning and run things during the day. Ross and Rand would still have the summers off when 80s Guys was the busiest.

In September, Ross and Rand were once again college students. Ross had changed his major to Marketing. Rand had changed his major to Business Management. They hoped to open up more restaurants like 80s Guys someday. They both felt great to be back on the campus at Weber State University. It hurt a little the first time they walked by the duck pond, where they walked with Cindy and Sandy on their first date. The Union Building also brought back memories of the twins after all the lunches with them while they were dating. A few weeks after they came back to Weber State, Ross and Rand no longer thought of the twins whenever they were in the Union Building or passed by the duck pond. They had truly moved

on. Life was good again.

Chapter Thirteen: Again?

Rand and Ross planned a Thriller theme night for Halloween in 1992. They decided to dress as zombies and walk around the restaurant, acting like the zombies from the legendary Michael Jackson music video Thriller. Halloween fell on a Saturday that year, and the restaurant would be packed.

The night before Halloween, Rand and Ross decided to return to the Friday Night Activity at the Ogden LDS Institute. The FNA was where they had first met and danced with Sandy and Cindy. Rand and Ross felt good about returning to the Institute. In fact, they looked forward to it. The scariest part of the night for the 80s guys was not being at the restaurant. Diamond Dave Paulsen had been doing a great job running 80s Guys when Rand and Ross were away at school, but they had never been gone on a Friday or Saturday night before. Even when they had dates on the weekend, they would start the date with dinner at the restaurant and then go out after closing time.

Rand and Ross were able to block the restaurant out of their minds. As difficult as it was to leave 80s Guys to someone else, they had a great time at the FNA. They danced all night. They heard and even enjoyed some nineties music. Lucky for them no grunge music was played. Rand and Ross could not have handled the dark period of rock music.

On the way home, they began to compare notes about who they had danced with at the FNA. "Out of all the girls I met tonight, one stood out to me. I danced with her a second time at the end of the night and then asked her if she wanted to hang out sometime. I got her number," Ross announced. "Do tell," Rand replied. Ross continued, "She is from North Carolina, and" Rand interrupted, "Wait! Do not tell me it happened again. Do not tell me we found identical twins again, or did we actually find the same girl this time." Ross looked at Rand incredulously and said, "You met her also? What are the chances?"

Rand pulled his truck into a Gas N Sip convenience store on Riverdale Road so he would not cause an accident. "How many girls were there tonight from North Carolina?" Rand asked. "I danced with Tiffany from North Carolina twice as well. I then asked her if she wanted to hang out sometime and then asked her for her number," Rand said with a bewildered tone to his voice. Did you say Tiffany? The number I have is from Debbie," Ross stated.

Ross then pulled Debbie's phone number out of his pocket. Rand also pulled Tiffany's number out of his pocket. Different names were written on each piece of paper, but it was the same phone number. "So, we found twins again, or maybe they are only sisters," Rand said again incredulously. "What are the chances?" Ross asked. "Describe Debbie," Rand asked. "She has dark hair and beautiful dark eyes. The kind you can get lost in. She was tall. Maybe 5'11, so almost as tall as me," Ross said. "Well, at least they are not identical twins. Tiffany has strawberry blonde hair and eyes of the bluest sea. She was tall, though, but more like 5'10," Rand said.

They both sighed in relief that they were not identical twins. Still, Rand and Ross needed to find out more about these two ladies. Are they twins? Are they sisters? "Do you have a quarter?" Ross asked. "I dropped one the other day. I think it is under my seat," Rand replied. Rand opened his door and looked underneath his seat. Sure enough, there was a quarter under there and more change totaling 84 cents. "There is a phone booth right there. We should give them a call," Ross said. It was now past midnight, but Rand and Ross needed their questions answered.

They walked over to the phone booth by the Gas N Sip. "You know, every time I come here, I see the same group of guys sitting and talking behind the store. I hear their conversations, and they are always about the same thing: women. If they know so much about women, what are they doing here at the Gas N Sip with no women around?" Rand asked. "It could be by choice," Ross replied.

Ross dialed Tiffany and Debbie's number. Debbie answered and said hello with a concerned sound in her voice. "Is this Debbie?" Ross asked. "Yes, this is Debbie," she replied. Ross began talking quickly so Debbie would not hang up because some guy she had just met was calling her after midnight, "This is Ross. We just met, but I have a friend named Rand who danced with someone from North Carolina. She gave Rand her phone number, and it is the same number. Are you two twins? Are you sisters?" Debbie giggled and was now much more at ease, "We are not related in any way, but we have known each other our entire lives and came out to Utah together to go to Weber State."

Ross high-fived Rand in the crowded phone booth. "Out of curiosity, why did you two decide to come to Weber State?" Ross asked. "My father played basketball at Weber State and loved his experience here. We wanted to experience something different than North Carolina, so here we are," Debbie replied. "So, do you like basketball?" Ross asked. "Of course, we are from the city that produced Michael Jordan," Debbie replied. Ross turned and high-fived Rand again. "You are from Wilmington, North Carolina?" Ross asked. "Yes, you know your basketball. I am impressed," Debbie replied. Ross high-fived Rand once again.

Rand could tell by the high-fives that the conversation was going well. He began nodding his head to encourage Ross, who now felt a bit emboldened. "Do you ladies have plans for Halloween? We run a restaurant called 80s Guys in Hooper, and we were wondering if you wanted to come out and spend Halloween in Hooper," Ross said.

"We have heard of that place. We heard it was a cool restaurant. A great atmosphere," Debbie replied. "We are the 80s guys in the 80s Guys restaurant," Ross commented. "You two are *the* 80s guys?" Debbie asked. "We sure are," Ross replied. "Hold on a second, please," Debbie said.

Debbie then covered the phone with her hand so she could talk with Tiffany. She came back thirty seconds later. Their phone, like most phones in the early nineties, was attached to the wall. There were no features on the phone that would allow you to mute your conversation, so holding your hand over the receiver was the only way you could "mute" your conversation. "We have been trying to figure out what to do tomorrow night. We were invited to a few parties, but we were unsure if it would be the right atmosphere. We both would love to come to 80s Guys tomorrow night. It sounds like fun," Debbie said. "Awesome! We have theme nights at 80s Guys, and tomorrow night is Thriller night. Have you seen the music video Thriller before? Ross asked. "Yes, we both love that video," Debbie replied. "With such short notice, we do not expect you to get dressed up," Ross said. "We will see what we can do," Debbie said. "We need to get set up tomorrow. Is there any way you ladies could meet us at the restaurant?" Ross asked. "That would be fine," Debbie replied. Ross then gave Debbie directions to 80s Guys, and they said goodbye.

Ross filled Rand in on everything Debbie had mentioned. "They are not twins, and they love basketball. Sweet!" Rand exclaimed. Debbie's dad played basketball at Weber State. How cool is that?" Ross added.

Rand and Ross worked all day on Saturday, first getting the restaurant ready for the Thriller theme night and then working on their zombie outfits. Even though they were both hard at work all day, they continually thought of their date that evening. They were both excited to spend some time with Tiffany and Debbie.

Tiffany and Debbie arrived at the restaurant around eight o'clock. Despite having less than a day to prepare, they did not disappoint with their costumes. They both came dressed as Michael Jackson's girlfriend from the music video. Debbie was dressed in a pink sweater over a white-colored shirt and a skirt, her hair in a ponytail tied with a white ribbon, like the girlfriend at the beginning of the video. Tiffany wore an outfit the girlfriend wore in most of the video. She wore capri-style jeans with a red shirt and a jean jacket over the shirt. She topped it off with high heels.

When the girls arrived, it was the first time Rand and Ross had stopped working all day. They gave the girls a tour of the restaurant and then took them into the arcade while they waited for a booth to open. Despite Rand and Ross having a lot of practice time on the video games, the ladies could hold their own. Tiffany even beat Rand at Space Invaders. That did not happen very often. After an hour in the arcade, the two couples were able to sit down. Everyone ordered Bono Burgers with Bon Jovi shakes. Rand was not worried about his stomach problems. He had learned to eat better and was in his element at 80s Guys. He was not overly nervous. The two couples watched Gremlins on the television closest to them as they waited for their food.

"What do you ladies like to do in your spare time?" Rand asked. "Spare time? We barely have any." Tiffany laughed. "Okay, what do you do with your time?" Rand replied. "Most of our time is spent in class, doing homework, and at our job nowadays," Tiffany said. "Where do you work?" Ross asked. "We both waitress at the Good Times Spaghetti Company in Ogden," Debbie said. "We used to play on their softball team," Rand mentioned. "We just finished a fall league playing on their co-ed team," Tiffany said. "Small world," Rand said. "So, you like sports?" Ross asked. "Absolutely, we grew up playing mostly basketball, but we were both injured our senior year," Debbie said. "Oh no, how did you get hurt?" Ross asked. "We both tore our ACL during the state playoffs in our first-round game. I tore my left, and Tiffany tore her right," Debbie responded. "That is horrible," Rand said. "We were undefeated and ranked first in the state. After we were both hurt, our team could not hold the lead we had built up, so we were bounced in the first round, and our dream of playing college basketball was over as well," Tiffany said. "We were being recruited by a lot of schools, including Weber State. Since my dad had played at Weber, we both leaned towards playing here. Our injuries were severe enough that we knew we could not play at that level again. We decided to still come to Weber anyway. We both received good academic scholarships, so here we are," Debbie added.

The more Rand and Ross listened, the more they liked what they heard. Now Ross was getting brave, "So you are beautiful, athletic, and smart," Ross stated. The two ladies blushed at that comment. Rand was not brave enough to say the same thing out loud, but he was certainly thinking the same thing. "Competitive too. I do not lose at video games often," Rand finally said.

"I am sure there are a lot of guys that ask you both for your number at FNAs," Ross said. "Actually, that was the first time we had ever gone to an FNA. We are always working on Friday nights. A pipe burst at Good Times on Thursday, so we are closed for a few days while they fix the pipe and repair the damage," Debbie said. "It must have been fate then," Ross said. "Yeah, we had not been to an FNA ourselves in several years," Rand added. "You have been busy with 80s Guys, I am sure," Tiffany replied. "That and we spent 1990 secluded in our rooms," Rand said before he realized this was not the best time to bring that up. Tiffany and Debbie looked at Rand and Ross quizzically, not knowing whether Rand was joking. "That is a story for another day," Ross said, saving the day for now.

The two couples talked and laughed until closing time. Rand and Ross both could make people laugh. After locking up, Rand and Ross took the ladies to a haunted house in Hooper. After arriving at the haunted house and getting out of the car, Rand started quoting Vincent Price's rap from Michael Jackson's song Thriller. "Darkness falls across the land. The midnight hour is close at hand. Creatures crawl in search of blood. To terrorize y'alls neighborhood," Rand said in a creepy voice. The haunted house scared both ladies, so much so that they grabbed Rand and Ross's hand through the scariest parts.

After the haunted house, the group drove back to 80s Guys to make hot chocolate. Rand felt some adrenaline from the haunted house, especially when Tiffany held his hand. "We should hang out some more," Rand said. Tiffany and Debbie both smiled. They clearly had fun. "We would love that. We were talking in the bathroom earlier and needed to figure out this busy schedule we all have. We all work on Friday and Saturday nights. We also have school and homework," Tiffany replied. Ross had an idea. "For now, how about we meet at the Union Building after our classes are over? We could eat lunch and then hang out and talk or play pool. Have either of you played pool before?" Ross asked. "We would kill you playing pool," Tiffany said with a smile. "There is that competitiveness," Rand said, also smiling. "Sounds like a plan," Debbie said. "We will see you in the Union Building cafeteria around 12:30 on Monday then," Tiffany confirmed.

Tiffany and Debbie then drove back to their apartment near Weber State's campus. After the ladies had driven off, Rand and Ross started high fiving each other. They then turned on some Bon Jovi to celebrate. "Bad medicine is what I need," they sang as Ross played the air guitar and Rand played the air drums. They were both excited. They had a great first date, and the girls also had fun. Rand and Ross knew the interest was mutual. When Rand mentioned hanging out again, Tiffany and Debbie had already discussed obstacles in seeing them again because they had busy schedules. They would not have been worried if there had been no interest in seeing Rand and Ross again. Life was good again.

Chapter Fourteen: We Used to be Hermits

The next Monday, Debbie and Tiffany met Ross and Rand in the cafeteria in the Union Building. They had lunch together. Rand always had to have a piece of cheesecake with his lunch, and this time, he shared a few bites with Tiffany. After lunch, they headed downstairs to play pool. Ross and Rand grew up with pool tables in their homes and played a lot in the Union Building. They both felt they were good at pool. As Tiffany predicted, the ladies destroyed Ross and Rand. "I hope they are not better than us at basketball," Ross told Rand.

That first day in the Union Building was the first of many days the foursome spent there together after they had completed their classes each day. The four always had lunch together and then played pool, video games, or bowled together. They had this routine for the rest of the Fall Quarter. Ross and Rand enjoyed getting to know Debbie and Tiffany in the Union Building.

Debbie's parents had met at Weber State. Her Mom had grown up in Ogden and went to Ogden High, just down the road on Harrison Boulevard. Her father grew up in Malad, Idaho, and went to Weber State to play basketball. They met each other in an English class. They dated, fell in love, and married before their Senior year at Weber State. After graduating from Weber State, Debbie's father, Jimmy, continued his education, eventually earning a doctorate in education from the University of Utah. Jimmy then taught at Salt Lake Technical College, now named Salt Lake Community College, before they moved so that he could teach at the University of North Carolina at Wilmington.

Tiffany's parents were high school sweethearts from Price, Utah. Tiffany's father, Jeff, played baseball at the College of Eastern Utah, now called Utah State University-Eastern, in Price and then finished his bachelor's degree at Utah State University in Logan. He attended graduate school at Idaho State University in Pocatello, Idaho, completing his doctorate there, and then taught at Salt Lake Technical College. Debbie and Tiffany's parents became friends when their dads taught at Salt Lake Technical College. Jimmy and Jeff both accepted teaching positions at UNC-Wilmington at the same time. The two families have been close ever since.

Debbie, Tiffany, and their siblings were the only members of the LDS church in their high school in Wilmington. Debbie and Tiffany both dated a lot in high school but only as friends. When they came to Weber State, they poured themselves into school and their jobs to pay their expenses. Ross and Rand were both impressed with how Debbie and Tiffany did not let obstacles stand in their way. They were not afraid to work hard to earn something. This drive did not lead to an active social life for the two ladies.

Debbie and Tiffany both had good academic scholarships at Weber State. Still, their scholarships did not pay for everything, such as room and board. What their scholarships did not cover, Debbie and Tiffany paid with their own hard-earned money. They had both overcome adversity by missing out on playing college basketball because of an injury. They did not let these obstacles stand in their way of achieving their goal of attending college.

As Thanksgiving approached, neither Debbie nor Tiffany had plans for it. This was Debbie and Tiffany's third year at Weber State, and the first two years, at Thanksgiving, they made a small dinner in their apartment near campus and then watched football together. Ross asked Debbie to eat Thanksgiving dinner with him and the Frasers, while Rand asked Tiffany to eat with him and the Brooke family.

The two couples had known each other for less than a month, but Thanksgiving was a big day in each relationship. Each couple spent more one-on-one time with each other. The Brooke family ate Thanksgiving dinner at Grandma's house every year. Rand's Grandma lived down the street from his parent's house. After dinner, Rand and Tiffany sat down with the rest of the family to watch football. The Dallas Cowboys played on Thanksgiving every year, and they were Tiffany's favorite team, too. They had a good team in 1992. A team that would win Super Bowl XXVII. Rand and Tiffany sat on a small sofa made for two in the back of the room.

Their conversation started with football, but after a while, Tiffany asked a question that had been on her and Debbie's minds since their first date. "You mentioned something about being secluded in your room for all of 1990 on our first date. Were you joking around, or what is that all about?" Tiffany asked. Rand took a deep breath. He knew he would have to discuss the twins and the aftermath sooner or later. Rand was hoping it would be much later. He scanned the room and decided that with the football game on and the conversations going on with his family, there was enough noise in the room for him to have a somewhat private conversation with Tiffany. Besides, it was not like his family did not know what had happened.

"Ross and I dated identical twins, we were engaged to them, they basically left us at the altar, we did not take it well, so we did not come out of our room for a year except to buy soda and potato logs once a day," Rand blurted out like he was in a race to see who could speak the fastest. Rand quickly realized he had talked too loud as everyone turned and looked at him, then turned back away. Tiffany's mouth dropped. She took a few seconds to regroup. "That is a lot to take in in just a few seconds," she said quietly. Rand's family were now looking at each other with wondering looks on their faces. They were not sure whether to leave and give them privacy or not. Rand began to speak again, but this time more quietly. His family stayed in the room and tried to ignore what was going on with Rand and Tiffany.

"I really like you, Tiffany," Rand said in almost a whisper. Rand continued, "I know it seems like I am this weird hermit guy right now, but yes, the whole thing with the twins threw me and Ross for a loop. Instead of taking the whole thing head-on, we swore off the nineties. We missed the entire Cincinnati Reds championship season, for crying out loud. We missed out on a lot of things. We just did not deal with it. Thank goodness for Ross's Uncle Brad and 80s Guys. Having the restaurant helped get us out of our funk. I could give you more details." Tiffany cut Rand off, "No, that is okay. I get it. You both were hurt bad."

Tiffany looked away for a few seconds as she contemplated her next words. "Are you over her?" Tiffany asked. Rand did not hesitate, "Yes, we met them at an FNA. The four of us hung out at the Union Building a lot together. I would not have been able to do those things with you if I were not over her. It would have brought back too many painful memories." Tiffany was taken aback to learn that Rand had met and spent time with this girl in a similar way as her. She looked down and pondered her next move. Rand could tell she was processing all this news.

Rand took solace in knowing Tiffany must have feelings for him, or she would have just blown this off. Rand decided not to speak to allow her time to process everything he had said. Rand acted as if he was watching the football game, but Tiffany was the only thing on his mind. After a minute of no words, Rand felt Tiffany's hand grab his hand. Even though they had spent a lot of time together in less than a month, this was their first display of affection other than holding hands at the haunted house on Halloween. Though Tiffany grabbed his hand on Halloween because she was scared not to show affection.

Tiffany leaned into Rand and said quietly, "I cannot imagine how horrible that would have been. I am sorry you had to go through it." Rand turned and looked at Tiffany. She was tearing up. "Thank you," Rand said. He then squeezed her hand a little tighter. Tiffany put her head on Rand's shoulder, and they finished watching the Cowboy's 30-3 victory over the Giants.

That evening, Rand and Tiffany walked out to the Great Salt Lake and watched the sunset over the lake. Just as the sun was setting, Rand noticed Tiffany getting cold. He pulled her in close to him. They both looked into each other's eyes. Then Rand gently kissed Tiffany. They kissed for a few seconds and then returned to looking into each other's eyes. Tiffany did not say anything. Rand did not say anything either because he knew he would likely say the wrong thing.

Rand grabbed Tiffany's hand, and they began walking back to his grandma's house. After walking for a few minutes, Rand broke the silence, "If I had to go back and go through that pain again so that I could be here, now, at this moment, with you, I would do it all over again." Tiffany stopped in her tracks and gasped. "That is the nicest thing anyone has ever said to me," Tiffany said. "Good, because I usually mess these things up by saying the wrong thing," Rand replied. Tiffany moved closer and kissed Rand.

When Rand and Tiffany returned, all the desserts were on the kitchen table and ready to eat. Rand's Grandma placed a giant piece of banana crème pie on a plate and handed it to Rand. She then asked Tiffany what kind she wanted. Tiffany replied, "Pumpkin pie is the best."

Rand shot her a grimacing look, "Ahh, our first fight. Nothing is as good as Banana Crème," Rand said. "Well, I will end our first fight by saying we must agree to disagree," Tiffany replied. After dessert, Rand and Tiffany left to meet up with Ross and Debbie at 80s Guys.

Ross and Debbie had a similar day to Rand and Tiffany. Thanksgiving dinner was at the Fraser home. After dinner, everyone sat down to watch football. Ross and Debbie sat down together on a large bean bag. Ross asked Debbie who her favorite team was. "I stick more with basketball. I cannot say that I have a favorite football team," Debbie replied. Then, today, you are a Dallas Cowboy fan," Ross said. I can live with that," Debbie remarked.

The comment Rand made on Halloween about 1990 had been on Debbie and Tiffany's minds since that night. They had discussed several times with each other about the comment and whether it was a joke. Like Tiffany with Rand, this was Debbie's first real chance to ask Ross about the comment. "I have been wondering about Rand's comment about being secluded in your rooms for all of 1990. I do not know Rand well enough to know if he was joking," Debbie said. "He jokes about a lot of things, but that was not one of them," Ross said solemnly.

Ross looked around and decided he had no choice but to discuss 1990. "Rand and I dated identical twins. We were engaged to them. We were going to get married in early January of 1990. Then they abruptly left and moved to Las Vegas. Elvis married them to two dudes, and apparently, they are dancers at a casino," Ross confessed.

Debbie's eyes were as big as the ocean. "You guys must have been crushed," Debbie said after catching her breath. "We were crushed, so crushed that we retreated to our rooms, swore off the nineties, and watched videotapes of MTV from the eighties" Ross remarked. "How long did that last?" Debbie asked. "1990," Ross replied. "You did not come out of your room for a year?" Debbie asked. "Once a day, we met at the Hooper Store to stock up on greasy food and soda. We also met once a month at Burger Bar. Burger Bar means a lot to us," Ross replied.

Debbie was stunned. She could not comprehend how this vibrant man before her had become a hermit for a year. "It is probably a good thing I did not know you then," Debbie said nervously with a small laugh. "Well, had you known and ran into us, you would not have recognized us with the long hair and beards. We looked like ZZ Top," Ross said. Debbie covered her face with her hands and laughed in her hands. "While I am throwing everything onto the table, we really stunk, too. Hygiene was not our friend in 1990," Ross said with a slight smile. The last comment made Debbie laugh harder, and she covered her face to lessen the noise.

Debbie stopped laughing, uncovered her eyes, and looked at Ross. They both looked into each other's eyes. "Looking back, I probably know you better in less than a month than I knew her after dating for almost a year," Ross said. Ross then looked around at his family, went back to looking into Debbie's eyes, and continued, "It hurt bad, but I am stronger having been through that trial. If not for that ordeal, there would be no '80s Guys, and I would not have met you." Debbie blushed, "Ahh, how sweet."

Ross and Debbie then sat quietly until halftime of the football game. "It is halftime. Let's go get some shots up," Ross said. "Now you are talking my game," Debbie replied. The couple walked outside to the basketball court in the backyard. Ross grabbed a basketball, and he and Debbie took turns shooting. After shooting and chatting, it got colder. "I should have worn my bigger coat," Debbie remarked. Ross sensed an opportunity. He walked over to Debbie and put both arms around her. "You are warm, Mr. ZZ Top," Debbie said, smiling. They both looked into each other's eyes, and then Ross kissed her. Debbie kissed him back, and the two could not think of anything more romantic than kissing on a basketball court.

Ross than asked Debbie, "If every rose has it thorn then what are your thorns?" Ross was referring to the popular eighties song "Every Rose has its Thorns" by Poison. Debbie grinned and said, "My jump shot is better than yours." Ouch! That is definitely a thorn in my side, Ross said.

After scoring on the court, Ross and Debbie retreated inside. They finished watching the Cowboys defeat the Giants, had dessert, and then headed to 80s Guys to meet up with Rand and Tiffany. On the short drive to 80s Guys, Ross reached out and grabbed Debbie's hand. "If everything I have been through the last three years had to happen for me to meet you, I am glad I went through it," Ross said. "That must have been horrible to endure, but I am glad we met each other, too," Debbie replied.

The foursome made hot chocolate and watched Christmas Vacation together. Watching Christmas Vacation to start the Christmas season had become a tradition for Ross and Rand. After the movie, Ross and Rand invited Debbie and Tiffany to attend church together at the Hooper Single Adult Branch on the coming Sunday. The 80s Guys and Good Times Spaghetti Company restaurants would be very busy the next two days. The ladies liked the idea of going to church together since, after a great day, they would not see Ross and Rand for the next two days.

After Debbie and Tiffany left, Ross and Rand filled each other in on their day. The men were too excited to sleep, so they listened to the Joshua Tree album by U2, one of their favorites. They talked as they listened to U2. "I feel like I know Debbie so much better than I ever knew Cindy," Ross said. "Dude, I know, it is crazy. I just love being around Tiffany. I did not want today to end," Rand added. "I've thought that maybe I should slow down after what happened before, but I think so much of Debbie. This is different," Ross said. "I am impressed that they earned a scholarship and are paying for the rest of their college. They work hard at their jobs. They have had adversity in their lives, with them both tearing their ACL and losing out on playing college basketball. This does feel different," Rand added.

Debbie and Tiffany attended church with Ross and Rand that Sunday at the Single-Adult Branch. This was another important step in both relationships. Ross and Rand were convinced that Debbie and Tiffany had learned values in their lives—values that Cindy and Sandy had not learned yet. Looking back, Ross and Rand had not concerned themselves with whether Cindy and Sandy had developed testimonies of the Savior and his Atonement, Joseph Smith, and the Restoration. They were not going to make that mistake with Debbie and Tiffany.

After the three-hour block, the two couples split up for Sunday dinner. Ross and Debbie ate at Ross's parents' home, and Rand and Tiffany ate at his Grandmother's home like they did on Thanksgiving. Rand's Grandmother asked, as she always does, what everyone learned at church that day. Everyone at the table had a Thanksgiving lesson that day. The discussion turned to what everyone was thankful for. Tiffany listened to everyone, and then, when there was a short break in the discussion, she spoke up and said, "I am thankful for my Lord and Savior, and I have parents who taught me about the Gospel of Jesus Christ." Rand's Grandmother smiled and said, "What a great testimony Tiffany."

The entire room was smiling at Tiffany. The biggest smile in the room belonged to Rand. He then thought about how thankful he was that Tiffany came into his life. Also, for his Grandmother's mashed potatoes and gravy.

Ross and Debbie finished their Sunday dinner and retreated to the bean bag in the family room. "I loved Michael Moulding's lesson today," Debbie said as they sat down. "Yeah, he puts a lot of effort into his lessons," Ross replied. "I kept thinking about how great the Gospel of Jesus Christ is and how lost I would be without it. When Tiffany and I came out here on our own to go to school, work, and try to get good grades, I knew we would be okay because of the church. I know it is not the same as going to a foreign country and serving a mission, but it was hard for us," Debbie said. "On a mission, we have a companion, church members, study time, and a structure that helps us stay on track. You and Tiffany had each other, but besides that, you had to figure it out on your own. That is very impressive to me," Ross replied.

Later that night, after Debbie and Tiffany had gone home, Ross and Rand recapped their day. "I am just so impressed with Debbie's testimony," Ross said. "Yea, my family was blown away with Tiffany. I am glad we saw this side of the two of them," Rand added.

The next day, classes were once again in session at Weber State. The two couples were back to their schedule to meet for lunch at the Union Building, and Ross and Rand still lost at pool to Debbie and Tiffany most of the time.

All four were busy with schoolwork to finish the quarter and their jobs. Free time was rare, so phone calls were sometimes the only chance to communicate besides their weekday lunch dates. Ross loved to hear Debbie's voice, as did Rand with Tiffany.

As Fall Quarter came to an end, Debbie and Tiffany made plans to return to North Carolina for Christmas. They booked their flights for the day before Christmas. Debbie and Tiffany would return five days later so they could work before the Winter Quarter of 1993 started. Ross and Rand had some quality time with their ladies before they left for North Carolina. They spent their time shopping, watching Christmas movies, and talking.

The five days Debbie and Tiffany spent in North Carolina seemed very long to Ross and Rand. They spoke every day on the phone and ran the phone bill up at 80s Guys. Debbie gave Ross some surprising news just before returning to Utah. "My parents are flying out to Utah the second week of January. My dad says he wants to see a few Weber State games, but I really think he wants to check you out," Debbie told Ross. "Oh, that sounds like fun," Ross replied, trying to hide the nervousness in his voice.

Rand laughed when Ross told him the news that Debbie's parents would be visiting. "Dude, if that was me, I think my stomach issues would be returning," Rand said while giggling. The joke was soon on Rand. When Tiffany returned to Utah, she told Rand that her parents would visit the third week of January. "I guess the good news out of this is the ladies must have talked about us enough to their parents that they feel they need to come here to see what we two dudes are all about," Rand said, grabbing at his stomach.

Before any parents visited, there was New Year's Eve to celebrate. 80s Guys was busy as ever on New Year's Eve until well after ten o'clock. Ross and Rand decided to clean up later, so they scurried over to pick up Debbie and Tiffany, who worked just as late. The two couples made it over to Weber State for the New Year's dance just twenty minutes to midnight.

Just before midnight, Ross told Debbie about a Weber State tradition called the True Wildcat. "If you kiss someone under the Bell Tower at Midnight on New Year's, then you become True Wildcats," Ross said. "Sounds great. Let's do it," Debbie replied. Debbie told Tiffany what they were up to, and she and Rand decided to join.

The two couples positioned themselves under the Stewart Bell Tower just before midnight but on opposite sides. Once the clock struck midnight, kissing ensued under the clock tower. "Now that I think of it. It is midnight on Homecoming, not New Year's," Ross confessed. "I knew what you were up to, Ross. I know all about the True Wildcats tradition. My parents became True Wildcats together. I am not complaining, though," Debbie admitted as she kissed Ross again. Tiffany knew the actual method of becoming a True Wildcat as well. "You guys are so slick. Except we both knew what you were up to. I cannot wait for Homecoming now, though," Tiffany said when Rand admitted to their scheme.

All four were back at Weber State for the Winter Quarter the next Monday. They also followed the same weekday routine of classes in the morning, lunch, and hanging out in the Union Building, as well as work and homework in the afternoon and evening. Debbie and Tiffany attended church in Hooper with Ross and Rand every Sunday now. The two couples liked going to church together, and they also enjoyed spending some time with Ross and Rand's families after church.

Debbie's parents arrived in Utah mid-week in the second week of January. Debbie was able to get Wednesday and Thursday off that week. The first night, they would spend at 80s Guys and then attend Weber State's Men's Basketball game on Thursday. Debbie's parents, Jimmy and Heidi, arrived along with Debbie at dinner time. Ross had some Bono Burgers ready to go when they got there. After dinner, Ross gave them a tour of the arcade and restaurant. Jimmy spent a few dollars playing Frogger and Donkey Kong. Then, all four found a booth again and chatted for a while.

"You have a real fun place here, Ross," Heidi said. "Thank you. It has been a lot of fun for us, especially here in our hometown," Ross replied. "You ever play any George Strait here?" Jimmy asked. "On Monday nights, we do. Monday night is country night. We just started that tradition. It is a big hit here in Hooper," Ross replied. "Have you seen George Strait's new movie?" Heidi asked. "No, I have wanted to take Debbie to see it, but with our schedules, it has been hard to get out at night. We mainly see each other during the day at school and now on Sundays," Ross replied.

Ross realized the more he talked with Debbie's parents, the more comfortable he felt around them. They were both very down-to-earth. After chatting some more, it was late, so Debbie took her parents to their hotel. The next night, Debbie went to Weber State's Men's Basketball game with her parents. Many staff and fans recognized Jimmy, and they were excited to see him. Jimmy was able to catch up with a few former teammates at the game.

Debbie needed to work on Friday night, so her parents had a free night without any set plans. They decided to have dinner at 80s Guys. Ross was surprised but glad to see them. "We loved it here so much on Wednesday that we decided to come back," Heidi said when they were greeted by Ross. Ross took good care of them again. Jimmy once again took another shot at Frogger and Donkey Kong in the arcade. Jimmy and Heidi stayed for a couple of hours. As they left, Ross thanked them for coming back. "Well, we really enjoy it here. We also like talking with you, Ross. Debbie has never had a boyfriend before. When she was home, she never stopped talking about you. We felt like we knew you before we met you," Heidi said. Jimmy nodded his head in agreement.

Debbie worked again the next night, but there was a Weber State home game again. Jimmy and Heidi attended the game without Debbie and once again enjoyed catching up with former teammates and others they had known in college. Jimmy and Heidi came down to Hooper and went to church at the Single-Adult Branch. They stayed for the entire block. "The Spirit is strong in this Branch," Jimmy remarked.

After church, Jimmy and Heidi ate dinner at the Fraser home. After dinner, the two sets of parents, along with Ross and Debbie, sat and talked in the family room. Ross and Debbie sat together on the big bean bag. "Your parents are meeting my parents. This must be getting serious between us," Ross needled Debbie. "I thought it already was serious," Debbie replied with a big smile on her face.

Jimmy and Heidi flew back to North Carolina on Monday morning. Debbie did not work on Monday night, so she surprised Ross at 80s Guys after getting some homework done. Ross was nervous about meeting Debbie's parents but ended up enjoying their stay. He was glad to see Debbie when she dropped in because they had not been alone since before her parents came.

After closing, Debbie helped Ross clean up. They found themselves alone back in the kitchen. Ross grabbed Debbie and pulled her close. He looked into her eyes for a second and then kissed her. "I have missed that," Debbie said with a smile on her face. "Me too," Ross replied. "You made a big impression on my parents. Almost as big an impression as you have on me," Debbie said, still smiling. Ross reached out and caressed Debbie's cheek and then kissed her again. "I have fallen in love with you, Debbie. I should be scared after what happened before, but I feel so secure when I am with you," Ross said warmly. Debbie's eyes began to moisten. "It is interesting that I could not get a Friday night off with my parents in town, but because of a broken pipe, I had a Friday night off when we met. I love you too," Debbie said. They kissed again. Life was so good.

Tiffany's parents, Jeff and Stephanie, planned a similar trip as Debbie's parents did the week before. They would fly into Utah on Wednesday and then fly back to North Carolina the following Monday. Ross did not say much to Rand about his time with Debbie's parents, other than it went well. Ross had been nervous before Jimmy and Heidi's visit and Rand was super nervous about Tiffany's parents' visit.

Jeff and Stephanie, along with Tiffany, visited 80s Guys restaurant on their first night in town. Rand gave them a tour when they arrived. Jeff's game was Galaga, and he spent three dollars in the arcade playing it. Each game was only a quarter, so Jeff played twelve games. When Jeff emerged from the arcade, his daughter asked him if he was trying to beat her high score. "You are just mad because you cannot beat me at pool," Jeff replied to Tiffany. Rand thought to himself that he better not ever play against Jeff in pool if he is better than Tiffany.

When a booth became available, Rand sat down with Tiffany and her parents. Bono Burgers were ordered for everyone. Jeff watched a music video on one of the screens. "The best drummer I have ever seen was Jay Osmond. We saw the Osmonds this last summer in Branson, Missouri, and he was unbelievably good with the sticks," Jeff said. "I have heard more than once that Jay Osmond was a fantastic drummer," Rand added.

Tiffany got up and said she needed to use the restroom. Rand gave her a "what are you doing to me" look. Tiffany whispered in Rand's ear, "They do not bite." Jeff started talking as soon as Tiffany walked away. "This is a great place you got here, Rand. All Tiffany talked about when she was home for Christmas was you and all you have going on here," Jeff said. "Really, she talked about me?" Rand said with glee in his voice. Jeff and Stephanie gave Rand a quizzical look. "We thought you knew how much she liked you," Stephanie said. "You are the first boyfriend she has ever had. I guess I am not her favorite guy anymore," Jeff said as he chuckled.

At this point, Rand could have floated home, but technically, since he lived at 80s Guys, he was already home. When Tiffany returned, Rand could not stop smiling at her. "You are a whole lot happier than before I left," Tiffany said softly so her parents could not hear. "Yes, I am," Rand said with a smile.

The next day, Jeff and Stephanie set out for Price, which was approximately two and a half hours away, to see family there. Jeff and Stephanie's parents had retired and moved away from Price. Jeff's parents had moved to Queen Creek, Arizona, while Stephanie's parents had moved to St. George, Utah. However, both Jeff and Stephanie had siblings in the area. They would spend Thursday and Friday in Price and return to the Ogden area on Saturday morning.

Jeff and Stephanie spent the day with Tiffany and shopped at the Ogden City Mall. Tiffany had to work on Saturday night. With a free night without Tiffany, Jeff and Stephanie decided to surprise Rand at 80s Guys. "We loved it here so much we wanted to come back," Stephanie said as they were greeted by Rand. "I wanted another shot at Tiffany's high score on Galaga as well," Jeff said. Jeff would spend five more dollars playing Galaga that night and still could not beat Tiffany's high score. "I think he really likes the Bono Burger, too," Stephanie commented.

While Jeff shot giant flies with a spaceship, Rand and Stephanie talked at a booth. "I do not mean to pry, Rand, but do you see yourself doing this the rest of your life?" Stephanie asked. "I love doing this, especially in our hometown. Yeah, if we continue to have success and fun doing it, I could see myself doing this for the rest of my life. Ross and I changed our majors with the idea that we would try to make the restaurant business our career. We have thought about opening another one someday, maybe in Kaysville. We have something special here, so we do not want to water it down by putting 80s Guys all over the place. We may try a different theme. I really like the eighties though," Rand replied. "It is rare to be able to do something you love for a living, Rand," Stephanie commented. "Can I ask you a question?" Rand asked. "Anything," Stephanie replied. "What does Tiffany think about the restaurant? We have never talked about a future together. I do not want to scare her off," Rand said. "I do not think there is anything you could do to scare Tiffany off. She is so smitten with you, Rand. I have never seen her like this. She knows you love this place, and she thinks it is great," Stephanie replied. Rand was smiling and blushing at the same time. "She is smitten with me. Wow, I feel like Lloyd Dobler after his first date with Diane Court," Rand cried. "*Say Anything* is a good movie," Stephanie replied. "Those guys behind the Gas N Sip are hilarious," Stephanie continued.

The next day, Jeff and Stephanie attended church in Hooper with Rand and Tiffany. Afterward, they went over to Rand's Grandmother's house. They had Rand's favorite mashed potatoes and gravy. Rand's Grandmother had also made an incredible pot roast. Jeff and

Stephanie had never seen the Great Salt Lake up close, so after dinner, they walked to the shores of the Great Salt Lake with Rand and Tiffany. It was cold, but still a beautiful sunset.

Jeff and Stephanie flew back to North Carolina the next morning. Later that day, after lunch in the Union building, Rand and Tiffany took advantage of the warm weather they had had for a January and walked around the Duck Pond. "I loved spending time with your parents," Rand said. "I believe they were quite smitten with you as well," Tiffany replied. "Smitten? I like that word," Rand said with a big grin on his face.

Rand grabbed both of Tiffany's hands and faced her so he could look into her eyes. "I love you, Tiffany," Rand said softly. Tiffany smiled and closed her eyes. When she opened them back up, they were as wet as the snow on the ground. "I love you too, Rand," Tiffany replied. They kissed softly. A car driving out of the nearby parking lot honked. Neither Rand nor Tiffany budged at the horn. They just gazed into each other's eyes. Life was so good.

Chapter Fifteen: First-Time Customers

In March of 1993, Rand and Ross had two waitresses at 80s Guys who left to try and make it as country singers in Nashville. Rand and Ross just so happened to know a couple of very qualified waitresses in Tiffany and Debbie. It was a win-win for all four, with the two couples always looking to spend more time with their significant other. Tiffany and Debbie were also very familiar with 80s Guys, and Rand and Ross needed good waitresses as the summer months approached.

The two couples continued their weekday routines with lunch in the Union Building, and then to work. The only difference is that they all worked together. Tiffany and Debbie also continued to go to church with Rand and Ross in Hooper. The new work situation also allowed Rand and Tiffany, as well as Ross and Debbie, to have days off together so they could go on regular dates to the movies or watch a video together. Both couples were looking forward to taking advantage of that perk in the summer when they would not need to use their free time to study and do so much homework. Tiffany and Debbie wanted to graduate as soon as possible, so they stayed in Utah but took a lighter load in the summer.

Rand and Tiffany, as well as Ross and Debbie, had begun to discuss a long-term future together. Rand and Tiffany were in love with each other, and whenever they were apart, they could not wait to be back together again. Ross and Debbie likewise spent every second they could together.

The second Monday of June at 80s Guys started like every other summer day. Boys came in to play arcade games before and after baseball practice. Rand and Ross prepared the restaurant for a busy night. Being Monday, it was Country Night, and a good crowd was expected. Tiffany and Debbie came in at two and would work until closing.

Around 4:00, 80s Guys had two ladies walk in who had never been in 80s Guys before but had a lot to do with its existence. Tiffany greeted them and the girls asked if they could see Rand and Ross. Tiffany thought that was a bit peculiar. They did not look like salesman or anyone that would never drop by out of the blue. Tiffany then looked more closely at the two ladies. They were identical. Their long blond hair, their blue eyes, their height; everything was the same.

Tiffany froze as she realized Sandy and Cindy were in front of her. "Are they here or not?" Sandy asked with an annoyed tone. "Yes, I will go and get them," Tiffany replied. As Tiffany turned around, she saw Debbie standing behind the counter. Debbie had heard Tiffany and the girls' conversation and also realized these were *the twins*. Tiffany and Debbie looked at each other with sad, nervous faces.

As Tiffany walked past Debbie and back to the kitchen, many things were going through her head. The same things were going through Debbie's mind as well. Why are the twins here? Do they want Rand and Ross back? What would Rand and Ross do if they did? Will their feelings for the twins come back? What would that do to their relationship? Rand and Tiffany had never experienced a rocky point in their relationship. The same could be said for Ross and Debbie. How would their relationships make it through this?

Tiffany found Rand putting some silverware that had just been washed into a bin. "There is someone here asking for you, Rand," Tiffany said. Rand did not find that out of the ordinary. This happens every day. Had Rand looked up and gazed at Tiffany, he would have seen tears in her eyes.

Ross walked in the back door after taking some garbage out. "There is someone here to see you as well, Ross," Tiffany said. "Okay, let me wash my hands," Ross replied. Rand walked past Tiffany and through the swinging door that led into the restaurant with the bin still in his hands. After going through the door, he looked up to see Sandy standing in front of him, smiling. Rand dropped the bin, and the clanging of silverware hitting the floor could be heard in the kitchen. It was easily heard in the arcade over the video games, too. Ross finished washing his hands, and as he dried them, he yelled to Rand, "You have never dropped a pass in your life. What is the deal? You go dropping our clean silverware on the floor." Ross walked through the swinging door just in time to see Sandy reach out and grab both of Rand's hands. Ross then looked past them and saw Cindy standing behind Sandy.

Tiffany walked over and stood next to Debbie who was still behind the counter. They looked at each other with tears in their eyes and gave each other a nervous smile. Rand stood in silence when Sandy grabbed his hands. Sandy broke one hand off and pulled Rand with the other over to a booth. They sat across from each other. "I love this place, Rand. My parents told us about it. It is so cool," Sandy said. Rand finally spoke, "Yeah, we like it."

So many song lyrics were going through Rand's head. He thought of "King of Pain" by the Police, but then he thought he would have to change the lyrics to queen instead of king. His mind was going a million miles an hour. Then he thought of another song by the Police, "Don't Stand So Close to Me."

Sandy suddenly was the one that acted a bit nervous as she paused before speaking again. "I made such a mistake going to Vegas. It has turned into a disaster. We had to support our husbands because they kept losing their jobs. They drank away our money. I love to dance, but they asked us to do uncomfortable things. It was horrible," Sandy said. "I am sorry to hear that, Sandy," Rand replied softly. "Are you? I would think after what we did, you would be happy to hear that it was so bad," Tiffany said. "No, I would never want that for you," Rand replied. "Really? That means so much to me," Sandy exclaimed.

Sandy once again paused and acted nervous before speaking. "Can you give me another chance, Rand?" Sandy asked. Rand sat without speaking as he tried to find the right words. "We are going to change our ways. I want the life we were going to make for ourselves before we left. That was such a good plan you guys had," Sandy continued.

Rand again paused wanting to say the right things. Sandy believed that Rand was contemplating about them getting back together again. She reached out, grabbed both of hands and looked into Rand's eyes. Tiffany had been watching behind the counter until she saw Sandy grab Rand's hands again and look into his eyes. This was too much for her. She walked back into the kitchen and began to cry.

Rand wanted to say the right thing. No, there was no way he was getting back with Sandy. He loved the future he had planned with Tiffany. He loved her. He trusted her. All things he could no longer say about Sandy. Rand did not want to come across as bitter or judgmental, though. "Sandy, I think you are an amazing woman," Rand said. This made Sandy smile. Rand continued, "You have a wonderful life in front of you with a lot of happiness in store for you and a lucky man. That man will not be me, though."

Sandy dropped Rand's hands and immediately began to pout. "I hope you return to church, and I pray you find someone you can marry in the Temple one day. I really do want you to be happy, but I have met someone that makes me happy. I am sorry. Getting back on track and feeling the Spirit again. It is the Spirit that helped Ross and me after you and Cindy left. I know it will also help you and Cindy," Rand explained.

Sandy started to get angry, but she caught herself. The experiences in Las Vegas had matured her and Cindy. She knew she had made mistakes. Now, it was time to correct them and move on. "Thank you, Rand. Our time together was the best time of my life. I hope I can find someone like you. You always saw the goodness in me," Sandy said solemnly.

After Sandy had walked Rand over to a booth, Cindy grabbed Ross's hand and led him to a booth on the other side of the restaurant. Ross did not say anything. Cindy waited a few seconds after they sat down and began by saying, "I am so sorry about what happened. It was the biggest mistake of my life. Things in Vegas did not go well at all. Sandy and I are both divorcing our husbands" Cindy said. "I am sorry. I wish things had turned out better for you," Ross replied. "I was hoping you would say that you were glad it did not work out so that we could have another chance. I would do anything to go back and do things differently. I want to repent and get back on track." Cindy said with emotion in her voice.

Cindy reached across the table and put her hand on Ross's hand. Debbie was watching them from behind the counter. She almost walked back to the kitchen when Tiffany had left, but she wanted to keep an eye on Ross and Cindy. Seeing Cindy put her hand on Ross's hand hurt her deeply. She wondered how this woman could walk back into Ross's life and expect things to go back to the way they were. She also wondered if Ross would take her back. Debbie had finally had enough, and she left and walked back to the kitchen. She found Tiffany there, and the two embraced and cried in each other's arms.

Ross paused after Cindy told him she wanted to repent. He wanted to say the right thing. "I know our Savior lives. He paid for our sins and died for us so that we can repent and return to live with our Heavenly Father again. I do not know what happened in Vegas, but I know that you can repent, and your sins will be forgiven," Ross said humbly. Cindy smiled and looked hopeful. Ross continued, "I have met someone. I am in love with her." Cindy began to cry. "I know you can find that rod again and grab it. Never let it go. This will make you happy. I know this to be true. It was feeling the Spirit again that helped Rand and me get back on track when you and Sandy left," Ross added.

Cindy gathered herself and smiled at Ross. "Thank you, Ross. Our time together was the best in my life. I want you to be happy. I hope I can find someone like you someday," Cindy said. Ross and Cindy stood up and walked over to the front of the restaurant. Sandy and Rand were already standing there. Sandy and Cindy could tell from the look on each other's faces that they had had similar conversations. It was not what they wanted to hear, but it was what they needed to hear.

"Please tell your family hello and that I am sorry for all the anguish we caused," Cindy said to Ross. "Yes, please tell the Brookes hello, and I am sorry," Sandy added to Rand. Ross reached out and hugged Cindy just as Rand hugged Sandy. They smiled at each other, and then Sandy and Cindy turned and walked out of the restaurant.

After the twins had left, Rand and Ross turned and looked at each other. "I did not think that was on our calendar for today," Ross told Rand. "Not what I thought I would be doing when I woke up this morning," Rand replied. "We need to turn on some Bon Jovi, dude," Ross said with excitement. Rand began to sing, "You givvvvve love, a bad name." Rand and Ross began to play the air guitar and drums as they walked around the counter and put some Bon Jovi into the sound system. Rand and Ross had closure on the most difficult experience of their lives. Now, they were feeling good. They had the closure they needed, and they were both in love. Life is good.

"Where did the girls go?" Ross asked Rand. "Dude, they are probably wondering what is going on. They have no idea who we were talking to," Rand replied. Ross pushed open the swinging door to find Tiffany and Debbie crying in each other's arms. "Maybe they do," Ross said to Rand. Rand quickly followed Ross into the kitchen.

"Ladies, it is a great day for some Bon Jovi," Ross said loudly. Tiffany and Debbie looked up at Rand and Ross, who were smiling. "Yeah, what's up with the sad faces?" Rand added. Tiffany and Debbie just continued to look at the two men. Rand and Ross now decided to take a more mature approach. "I guess you figured out who the two women that just left were," Ross said. "The fact that they were identical twins, and they could not keep their hands off you two was a bit of a giveaway," Debbie shot back. "They are gone?" Tiffany asked. "Yes, they are gone," Rand replied.

Tiffany and Debbie continued to look at Rand and Ross while trying to figure out what was going on. "You sure do seem happy that they dropped by," Tiffany said. "I am glad they dropped by. We have closure," Rand replied. "Yes, we have closure, and honestly, it is good to know they are out of the situation in Vegas, and they want to try to get their lives back in order," Ross added. "They want to get back on track and go back to how things were with you guys. That was obvious," Debbie said, a bit snarky. "Maybe, but the part of them going back to their lives with us is not going to happen," Ross replied. Ross stepped towards Debbie and took her in his arms. He then looked into Debbie's eyes. "You are the only one for me," Ross said as he kissed her softly.

Tiffany walked towards Rand. "I was so scared I was going to lose you," Tiffany said to Rand. Tiffany hugged Rand. Rand whispered into Tiffany's ear, "When I said that I loved you, I meant that unconditionally. I love you and only you." Rand then kissed Tiffany. As Rand broke away from Tiffany he began to sing Journey. "I'm forever yourrrrrs, then pausing for dramatic effect, faithfully," Rand sang. Life was really good for both couples.

Chapter Sixteen: Life is Good

The twins dropping in had a big effect on the relationship of both couples. For Ross and Rand, it brought closure. After the twins went to Vegas, Ross and Rand could not go from being in love with Cindy and Sandy to completely not caring about them. That was what was so painful for Ross and Rand. They could have easily moved on if they did not care about Cindy and Sandy, but of course, they did care. After their breakups, Ross could not get the Def Leppard song, "Love Bites" out of his head. For Rand it was "With or Without You" by U2.

Now, Ross and Rand knew the twins were out of bad relationships and would have the chance to get their lives back on track. This made Ross and Rand happy that the two women they cared about had matured and would have a chance to repent and return to activity in the church.

Debbie and Tiffany were more secure than ever in their relationships with Ross and Rand. If there was ever a doubt about how Ross and Rand felt about them, those doubts were now gone. Debbie and Tiffany were confident in how much Ross and Rand loved them.

Before the twins' visit, the two couples had begun talking about the rest of their lives together. After the twins' visit, those discussions intensified. Neither couple wanted to wait much longer, so plans were set in motion.

In late June, Rand and Tiffany had a rare summer night off from 80s Guys. Rand took Tiffany to The Roof Restaurant, located on the 10th Floor of the Joseph Smith Memorial Building near Temple Square in Salt Lake City. As they waited for their dinner to be served at a table with a view of the Salt Lake Temple, Rand got down on one knee and proposed to Tiffany. After Tiffany said yes, the other diners gave the newly engaged couple a standing ovation.

After dinner, Rand and Tiffany held hands and walked around Temple Square. They decided on Friday, September 24, 1993, as their wedding day. They would take Fall Quarter off to get married and then settle into married life. They would then continue their work toward their bachelor's degrees in the Winter Quarter of 1994 at Weber State.

Rand stopped walking and looked into Tiffany's blue eyes. "I cannot imagine my life without you. I feel like my life began when I met you. I am the luckiest man alive," Rand said. "Oh, Rand, I love you so much. I am so happy," Tiffany replied. They kissed for the first time as an engaged couple.

A week later, it was Ross and Debbie's turn. Ross made a picnic dinner, and they had dinner at Beus Pond Park near Weber State. They sat down on a blanket, and Ross started getting the dinner he had prepared out of the picnic basket. He also pulled out a small boom box. Debbie thought Ross had prepared a mixed tape of their favorite songs to play as they ate a romantic dinner. Instead, Ross turned on the radio and tuned it to Weber State's campus radio station, KWCR. Ross knew one of the DJs for KWCR, who went by the name of Peace Dogg on air.

KWCR played hip hop music and the songs being played were not as romantic as Debbie had hoped. Then Peace Dogg began speaking between songs about a friend he knew who had met a special girl and had decided he wanted to spend forever with this special girl. "So, Debbie, Ross would like to know if you would marry him," Peace Dogg announced on air. As Peace Dogg made Ross's announcement, Ross pulled out a ring from the basket. Ross got down on a knee and then, in his own words, said, "Debbie, will you spend forever with me?" Through

tears in her eyes, she answered, "Yes." Peace Dogg played a romantic LL Cool J song as they

waited for the answer. Ross had borrowed a cell phone from his Uncle Brad and called into

KWCR. Debbie gave her answer on the air. Rand, Tiffany, and Ross's family were able to tune in

and listen to the proposal.

After they became engaged, Ross and Debbie held hands and walked around Beus Pond

Park. They decided on October 1 as their wedding date, one week after Rand and Tiffany's

wedding. This way, Debbie and Tiffany's families would be able to come out from North

Carolina and stay for both weddings.

As they walked, Ross stopped Debbie and took her in his arms. "You are the light of my

life, Debbie. I cannot imagine a life without you in it," Ross said. "I love you, Ross Fraser, with all

my heart," Debbie replied. They kissed and then stared into each other's eyes.

September 24th came quickly. There was so much to plan and get done in three months

that time flew by for Rand and Tiffany. They were married in the Salt Lake Temple for time and

all eternity. Their reception was held at Weber State's Sky Room in the Union Building. Before

the reception started, Rand and Tiffany snuck down to the pool tables. Rand was able to beat

Tiffany in pool, which rarely happened. Tiffany did not tell Rand, but she had decided for a

wedding present, she would let him win. For Tiffany to set aside her competitiveness was a big

deal.

The newly married couple honeymooned in London. Rand had a family friend that

allowed them to stay in their flat in the heart of London. It was a wonderful week for Rand and

Tiffany. They then flew back to Utah just in time for Ross and Debbie's wedding.

Ross and Debbie were also married in the Salt Lake Temple. Their reception was held in a room at the Dee Events Center, home of Weber State basketball. Debbie's dad loved the idea of having the reception at the Dee. The Dee Event Center was built after Jimmy's playing days, but Jimmy still loved being there. Ross had grown up going to games at the Dee along with Rand. The newly married couple honeymooned in Belize.

Each couple found small homes to rent in Hooper. All four continued to work at 80s Guys. When the Winter Quarter came around, they continued their studies at Weber State. Ross and Rand had decided they would continue to run 80s Guys after graduation. They thought about possibly expanding at some point. A friend from Hooper, Scott Kilts, had expressed some interest in investing in 80s Guys Restaurants. Kaysville might be a good spot to put the next 80s Guys. It was far enough away from Hooper that they could appeal to a new crowd but close enough to run both without too much running around.

Debbie and Tiffany had decided they would leave the restaurant business after graduation. Debbie wanted to become an English teacher and coach basketball. Tiffany hoped to teach History and coach basketball. Maybe Debbie and Tiffany would coach against each other someday.

Ross and Rand would forever stay loyal to the eighties. It was a great decade to be alive for with great music and movies. They would never accept the dark period of rock music known as grunge, but they now looked forward to the future. They would always look back at the eighties fondly while enjoying their current decade. Life was good.